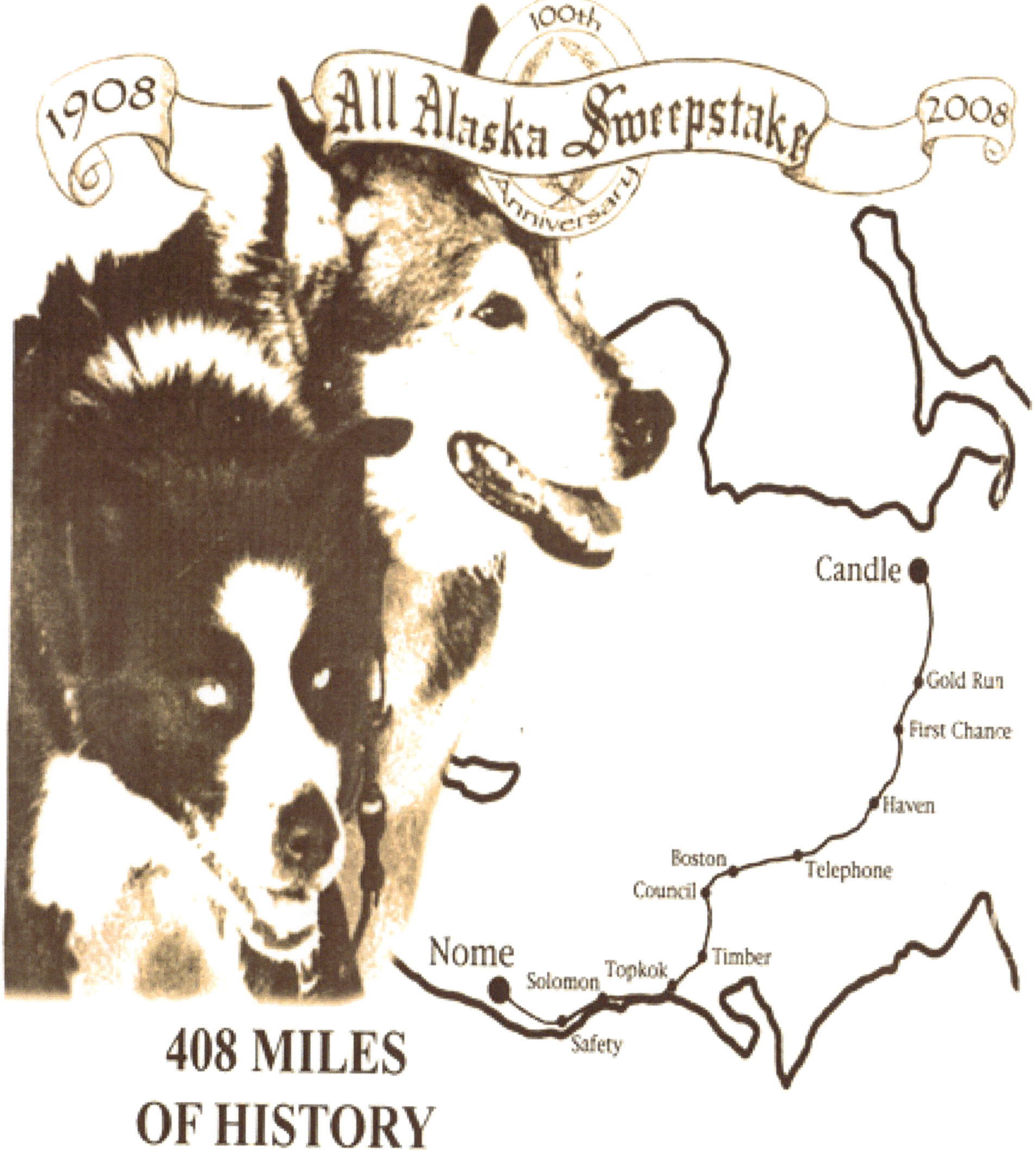
1908
All Alaska Sweepstakes
2008
100th Anniversary
Candle
Gold Run
First Chance
Haven
Telephone
Boston
Council
Timber
Nome
Solomon
Topkok
Safety
408 MILES
OF HISTORY

Trail marker and a sundog over the Bering Sea. Photo by Mark Hegener.

Sonny Lindner on the trail. Photo by Jan DeNapoli.

The All Alaska Sweepstakes

History of the Great Sled Dog Race • 1908-2008

by Helen Hegener
Photography by Jan DeNapoli
*Additional photos by Joe May, Donna Quante,
Mark Hegener, Sue Steinacher, Donna Morgan, June Price*

ALL ALASKA SWEEPSTAKES

All Alaska Sweepstakes
History of the Great Sled Dog Race • 1908-2008
by Helen Hegener

© 2010 by Northern Light Media.

All photographs in this book attributed to Jan DeNapoli are © 2008 Jan DeNapoli, Muzzy Graphics.

All photographs in this book attributed to Joe May are © 2008 by Joe May.

All photographs in this book attributed to Donna Quante are © 2008 Donna Quante, Husky Productions.

All photographs attributed to other photographers are © 2008 by those respective photographers.

Copyright under International and Universal Copyright Conventions. All rights reserved. No part of this book may be reproduced or transmitted in any form or by any means, electronic or mechanical, including photocopying, recording, or by any information storage and retrieval system, without written permission from the copyright holder, Northern Light Media. Brief passages not to exceed 500 words may be quoted for reviews of this book.

Hegener, Helen
All Alaska Sweepstakes: History of the Great Sled Dog Race • 1908-2008 / Helen Hegener
ISBN 978-0-984-3977-1-6
1. Alaska history. 2. Sled dogs.
Includes bibliography, resources, timeline and index.

To order single copies of this book please
send $24.00 plus $4.50 shipping
(U.S. addresses only) to the publisher:

Northern Light Media
Post Office Box 298023
Wasilla, Alaska 99629
http://northernlightmedia.com

Northern Light Media publishes books about sled dog history and races, and other books about the history of Alaska, including *Along Alaskan Trails: Adventures in Sled Dog History; Yukon Quest Album; Long Hard Trails and Sled Dog Tales;* and *The Matanuska Colony Barns: The Enduring Legacy of the 1935 Matanuska Colony Project.*

Lance Mackey's Dred at Council
photo by Jan DeNapoli

ALL ALASKA SWEEPSTAKES

The Start and Finish on Front Street in Nome. Photo by Jan DeNapoli.

This book is dedicated to the hardworking volunteers who made the 2008 Centennial Running of the All Alaska Sweepstakes a reality. They were there when it counted for the mushers, for the dogs, for the fans, and for each other.

ALL ALASKA SWEEPSTAKES

ALL ALASKA SWEEPSTAKES

"Early storms had covered the whole country with a soft white blanket of snow; but later, clear, cold weather had frozen the surface till the trails were in fine condition. They were smooth, with a crust that held..."
from Navarre of the North, by Esther Birdsall Darling (Doubleday & Company, 1930)

Right: Sunset in Council
Photo by Jan DeNapoli.

Opposite: Jeff King's frosty-faced team.
Photo by Jan DeNapoli.

ALL ALASKA SWEEPSTAKES

Mitch Seavey's team on the trail.

Opposite: Jeff Darling's dogs leave the starting chute. Both photos by Jan DeNapoli.

All Alaska Sweepstakes
History of the Great Sled Dog Race • 1908-2008

Introduction *"A Front Row Seat to History"*	**10**
Chapter 1: The History *"There's No Place Like Nome"*	**15**
Chapter 2: The Preliminaries *"$100,000 Winner Take All"*	**31**
Chapter 3: The Start *"Sixteen Teams Hit the Trail"*	**53**
Chapter 4: The Race *"Riding the Runners Through History"*	**83**
Chapter 5: The Finish *"Iron Man Johnson's 98-year Record"*	**109**
Chapter 6: The Legacy *"Celebrating the Centennial Running"*	**121**
Appendix & Bibliography *Additional details and resources*	**148**
Index *A complete index to the names, places, and items of interest*	**156**

ALL ALASKA SWEEPSTAKES

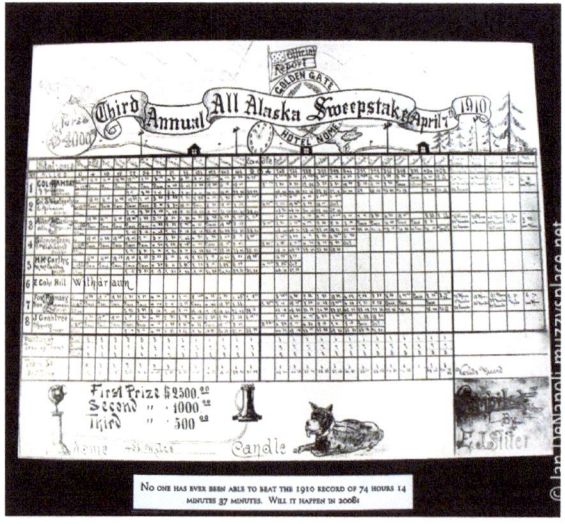

A Front Row Seat to History

by Helen Hegener

It's not often in life that one is unexpectedly presented with a front-row seat to history, but that was the offer made - and, of course, gratefully accepted - in early 2008, by my husband, Mark, and I. Our good friend and business associate, Donna Quante, had been invited to film the Centennial All Alaska Sweepstakes Race in Nome in March of that year, and to produce a documentary of the race. She asked if we wanted to join the media crew; Mark would be a second camera operator, and we would produce a commemorative book on the race. We'd already worked with Donna to produce our own documentary, *Appetite and Attitude*, about champion musher Lance Mackey, who had just won the 1,000 mile Yukon Quest for the third time, and who would win his second Iditarod just before taking on the historic All Alaska Sweepstakes.

The All Alaska Sweepstakes media team was headed by Theresa Daily, who'd been working with the race organizers for a long time. A recreational musher, Theresa had followed sled dog mushing for many years and had created and still maintained websites for many of the top mushers, including Lance Mackey. Her considerable skills as a graphics artist, a webmaster and a top-notch photographer had secured her a central place in reporting on sled dog races all across Alaska.

Donna Quante had moved to Willow, Alaska the year before after 35 years in broadcast television, working every type of production for the major networks and winning three National Emmy Awards for her camera work. She had produced a documentary, *Pretty Sled Dogs*, about the beautiful purebred Siberian Husky teams of Canadian musher Karen Ramstead, and she was working on other video projects when not training and running her own recreational dogteam. She'd done most of the filming for our documentary on Lance Mackey, and we had closely followed Lance in the Yukon Quest, from the halfway point at Dawson City to his third win in Whitehorse.

Talking with Lance on the trail, he'd told us more than once that his plans for that 2008 race season were to place in the top three in the Yukon Quest, and in the top ten in the Iditarod, but "I really want to win the Sweepstakes! It's only 400 miles and it's worth more than the other two put together!"

But he was always quick to add that even more than the richest payout in sled dog racing history, he loved the idea of adding his name to the Sweepstakes trophy with those venerable mushing legends, "Scotty" Allan and Leonhard Seppala.

Left, top Nome's oversized gold pan welcomes visitors.

Signpost in front of a local hotel.

1910 All Alaska Sweepstakes leaderboard.

All photos by Jan DeNapoli.

ALL ALASKA SWEEPSTAKES

"The 2008 Centennial All Alaska Sweepstakes was a one-of-a-kind event..."

Two more members of the All Alaska Sweepstakes media team joined us in Nome from the Fairbanks area: Jan DeNapoli, whose incredible photography was gaining attention all across Alaska; and Jodi Bailey, a champion musher whose masterful capabilities with math and spreadsheets were indispensible in tracking the race and maintaining an updated leaderboard.

The 2008 Centennial All Alaska Sweepstakes was a one-of-a-kind event not only for the mushers entered in the race, but for the army of volunteers who worked hard to ensure a smooth running: The race officials, veterinarians, pilots, and checkpoint crews; the handlers and trail support teams for each musher; the lovely ladies of the All Alaska Sweepstakes Queen contest, who raised money for the Finishers' Purses; the radio crews from the Seward Peninsula Amateur Radio Club; the planners and organizers of the wonderfully historic All Alaska Sweepstakes Awards Banquet; the coordinators for housing, race events, merchandising and advertising; all these people and many, many more came together to make this great historic race a reality.

As with any event of this magnitude, for every person whose name appears in this book, there are dozens of others whose names do not appear, but whose contributions were also an important part of the race effort. We sincerely hope this commemorative book gives each of them a reason to remember the magnificent Centennial All Alaska Sweepstakes Race with a smile.

See you at the next All Alaska Sweepstakes Race!

Mark Hegener, Johnny Johnson and Jodi Bailey in the comms room

Commenorative buckle awarded to the finishing mushers at the banquet

Board of Trade Saloon

A dog from Jim Lanier's team

Theresa Daily and her favorite dog from the Tuluksak team, Lewis

Mark Hegener in the dogyard

Nome's Board of Trade Saloon, on Front Street, site of the All Alaska Sweepstakes founding. Photo by Jan DeNapoli.

Top: Nome Kennel Club pennant. Photo: Jan DeNapoli. Bottom: Leaderboard, 1912 Sweepstakes race. Photo: Joe May.

ALL ALASKA SWEEPSTAKES

"On a cold spring day in 1907 a group of us gathered around the stove in a Nome saloon and began talking about dog races. After a few weeks of arguing we worked out the rules of the 'All-Alaska Sweepstakes.' Beginning with the spring of 1908 this great race of dog teams was run every year until the war, the last one in 1917. It became world-famous, and has set the pace for every important dog race since."
A.A. ("Scotty") Allan, in Gold, Men and Dogs (G.P. Putnam's Sons, 1931)

1910 Nome newspaper, from the Carrie McLain Museum, photo by Donna Quante

Chapter One: The History

"As I see it, such races will become a permanent thing in Nome. We all know what an important part dogs have contributed to the development of Alaska, how dependent we are up here on them for transportation. I propose that we establish a Kennel Club, the purpose of which will be to improve the strains of Alaskan dogs, and to better their conditions. The Annual All-Alaska Sweepstakes races...will serve to prove which dogs are best. I predict that dog racing in Alaska will prove as popular a sport as horse racing in Kentucky."
-Albert Fink, Nome lawyer and first President of the Nome Kennel Club, established 1907 at the Board of Trade saloon, Nome, Alaska

Satin purse bag in the gold and green colors of the Nome Kennel Club from the 1910 race, which contained $10,000 in gold coin; it was won by the Colonel Charles Ramsay dogteam. On display at the Carrie McLain museum in Nome, photo by Donna Quante

ALL ALASKA SWEEPSTAKES

100 year Legacy: The World's First Organized Sled Dog Race Was The All Alaska Sweepstakes

Crowd at the 1908 All Alaska Sweepstakes. In her 1929 novel 'The Trail Eater,' Barrett Willoughby describes the scene: "In front of the judges' stand racing drivers were already swinging their teams in--lines of superbly trained, lithe-limbed, thin-flanked dogs, groomed to a hair and stripped to their twelve-ounce racing harnesses. At every new arrival a cheer burst from the watching crowd, a cheer that was both for the dogs, and for their tense-faced driver standing behind the handlebars, furred, mukluked, with his starting number on a white square sewed to the front and to the back of his parka."

The souvenir booklet of the second annual All Alaska Sweepstakes, run April 15, 1909. A Norwegian immigrant named Louis Thrustup drove a team in that race which was owned by a Russian fur trader, William Goosak, and comprised of dogs from Goosak's homeland, Siberia. They were smaller and lighter than the typical large freighting dogs which the miners and mailteam drivers were running in the Sweepstakes races, and they garnered much attention from spectators and mushers alike.

John "Iron Man" Johnson's team, 1912. In the 1910 race Johnson drove a team for the Scottish nobleman, Fox Maule Ramsay, who had traveled to the Anadyr River area of Siberia and brought back to Nome around sixty of the "thick-coated, prick-eared, tough-footed, swift little foxy-looking dogs," which became the distant forerunners of today's Siberian husky.
Driving a team of these speedy little huskies, with his own blue-eyed Siberian leader Kolyma in front, Johnson set a record in the 1910 race of 74 hours, 14 minutes, and 37 seconds. It was a record which stood until 2008.

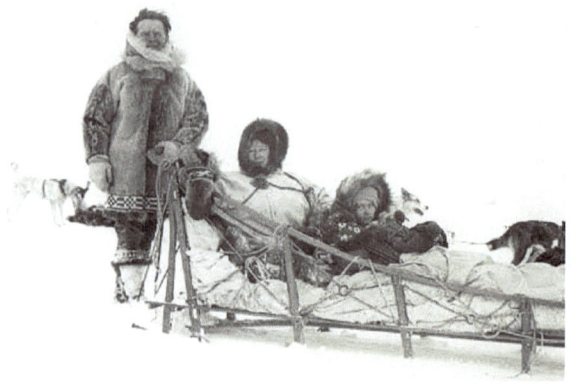

The great dog driver Leonhard Seppala around the time of his first All Alaska Sweepstakes race, in 1914, posing with his wife, Constance, and their daughter Sigrid. A legend in his own time, Seppala lost the first race when he miscalculated the trail, nearly losing his team - and his life - over cliffs which rimmed the Bering Sea. Sliding on ice, barely twenty feet from disaster, his freighting leader Suggen, half Siberian and half malemute, clawed his way to safety with a young and inexperienced team scrambling behind him. Later Seppala said, "I don't know what [Suggen] told them, but it worked."

All Alaska Sweepstakes Check Point History 1908-1917

- **Nome** Start & finish
- **Fort Davis** (3.5 miles) also know as Nome River in 1912 & 1914. Galvin's in 1911.
- **Hastings** (9.1 miles) Check point in 1908-1911, 1913.
- **Cape Nome** (13 miles) Check point for all of the years.
- **Safety** (22 miles) Check point for all of the years.
- **Solomon** (33 miles) Check point for all of the years.
- **Topkok** (47.2 miles) A check point from 1908-1913.
- **Timber** (59.7 and 67 miles, depending upon report)
- **Council** (75-85 miles depending upon report) Check point for all of the years.
- **Baker's** (89 miles) Check point for 1912, only.
- **Boston** (95.6 miles) Check point 1910 through 1917.
- **Fish River** (121 miles) Check point in 1916 only.
- **Telephone** (110 – 125 miles depending upon report) Check point 1908-1915.
- **Haven** (124-143 miles depending upon report) Check point for all years.
- **First Chance** (165 miles) Check point for 1908, 1909, 1910 and 1911.
- **Gold Run** (176 miles) Check point for 1912-1917
- **Candle** (204 miles) Check point and halfway point for all years of the race.

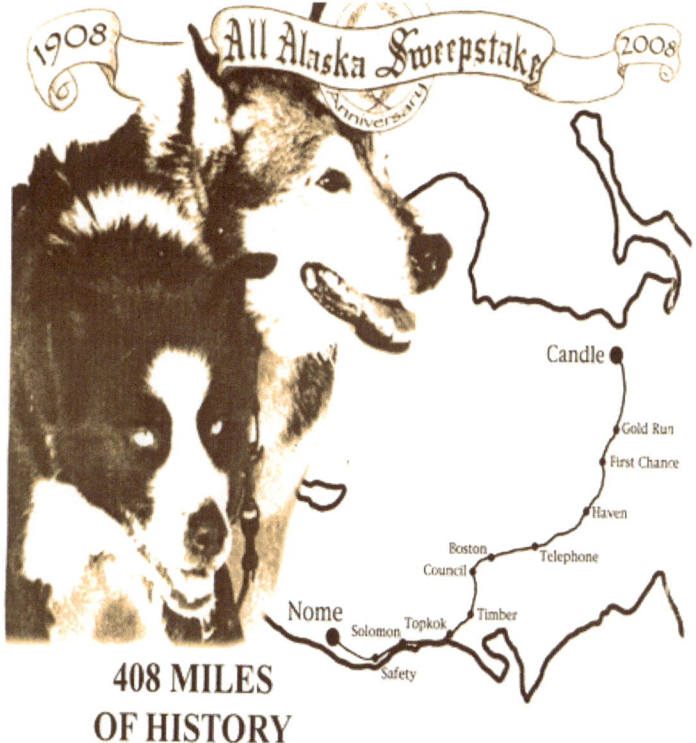

408 MILES OF HISTORY

Allan Alexander "Scotty" Allan

Scotty Allan wrote in his autobiography Gold, Men and Dogs (1931, G.P. Putnam's Sons), "It was great fun winning a race. No matter how much you suffered you felt all right in the end; the same applied to the dogs. The toughest job of all was to go through with a race which you lost. You not only had the disappointment, but the dogs always seemed to know that things hadn't gone right."

Scotty tells of the harrowing 1910 race when he literally "fell off a mountain," when a snow ledge gave way beneath his team and he and his team rolled over two hundred feet down a nearly vertical drop, but they gathered themselves and finally arrived at the finish line with "five dogs hitched, two in the sled, and three tied behind."

Scotty later wrote that the last three and one half miles of the race were a total blank, "I never remembered any of it afterwards." And he didn't remember tying the three loose dogs to his sled.

ALL ALASKA SWEEPSTAKES

SCOTTY AND BALDY

The Trail Eater

Barrett Willoughby's novel *The Trail Eater: A Romance of the All Alaska Sweepstakes* (1929, G.P. Putnam's Sons) featured a hero based on the real Scotty Allen. The foreword to her book captures the legend of the race: "In this novel of love and reckless adventure I tell of the gold town of Nome in the heyday of its glory--rich, careless, luxurious, and ugly. Nome in evening clothes and on the trail. Nome where the wolf-dog was king, and fortunes were lost, and gold mines were won on strings of racing malemutes. I tell of the Sweepstakes Trail, and the daredevil drivers who risked their lives on that four-hundred-mile course that is the longest, most hazardous, most cruel--and most fascinating--known to the world of sport. My characters are fictional, but every racing incident is drawn from the colorful career of the champion driver of the All Alaska Sweepstakes--Allen Alexander Allan."

The History of the All Alaska Sweepstakes

In their ground-breaking book on the 1925 diphtheria epidemic in Nome, titled *The Cruelest Miles,* cousins Gay and Laney Salisbury set the stage and describe turn-of-the-century Alaska: "From the beginning, Nome depended on its dogs. Teams were drafted into service as mail trucks, ambulances, freight trains, and long-distance taxis. The demand for sled dogs was so high, particularly in the northern gold rushes, that the supply of dogs ran out and a black market for the animals sprang up in the states. Any dog that looked as if it could pull a sled or carry a saddlebag-whether or not it was suited to withstand the cold-was kidnapped and sold in the north."

Skilled and experienced dog drivers quickly gained reputations, and by his frequent travels and exploits, A.A. "Scotty" Allan became known throughout the territory as a dog man of the highest caliber. He was reputedly able to train even the most surly dogs and press them into reliable service, and it was his young son George who originally proposed a race to resolve the question of whose dogs were the fastest in Nome. George and his young friends organized a race which George won with a dog who, years later, would later become famous around the world: the incomparable Baldy.

The Salisbury cousins explained Scotty Allan's place in the context of the sweepstakes races: "In the first years of the sweepstakes, Scotty Allan won most of the races, and for years his teams were considered Alaska's top dogs. Allan had a natural gift with animals and had trained horses and dogs since he was a twelve-year-old in Scotland. To prepare for the sweepstakes, he experimented with the dogs' diets and spent hours in the kennels examining the paws of each dog, trimming the claws so they would not catch in the snow, and greasing the pads. He made rabbit-fur covers for his team, which had shorter hair than most of the local dogs, and designed booties for their feet, which were more tender and prone to injury. He designed racing harnesses that were lighter and less cumbersome and made the traditional freight sled lighter and replaced its handlebars with a crossbar that made it easier to push. His basic designs are still in use today."

The course set for the All Alaska Sweepstakes was a tough one, traversing the width of the remote Seward Peninsula from south to north and back again. Esther Birdsall Darling described the trail in her promotional booklet and Official Souvenir History, *The Great Dog Races of Nome*: "The route varies consistently - from hour to hour - from narrow passage between towering ice hummocks of the Bering Sea to wide plains of unbroken snow; from the steep slopes of Topkok Hill, to the desolate, storm-swept waste of Death Valley; from the pleasant winding road through wooded Council district, to the trackless and treacherous ice on rivers and lakes."

Archdeacon of the Yukon Hudson Stuck explained a goodly bit about the country in his 1914 book, *Ten Thousand Miles with a Dogsled*: "Traveling, like so many other things, is very different on the Seward Peninsula. The constant winds beat down and harden the snow until it has a crust that will carry a man anywhere."

A little later, after describing the local meteorological peculiarities, he continues: "So a striking difference in travel at once manifests itself; in the interior all the snow is soft except on a beaten trail itself, while in the Seward Peninsula all the snow is alike hard. The musher is not confined to trails-he can go where he pleases; and his vehicle is under no necessity of conforming in width to a general usage of the country-it may be as wide as he pleases. Hence the hitching of dogs two and three abreast; hence the sleds of twenty-two, twenty-four, or twenty-six inches in width. My tandem rig aroused the curiosity of those who saw it. Hence many other differences also."

And of the trail from Candle to Council the Archdeacon wrote: "For a while there would be travel such as one sees in children's picture-books, where the man sits in his sled and cracks his whip and is whisked along as gaily as you please - such travel as I had never had before; but there was no pleasure in it - the wind saw to that."

ALL ALASKA SWEEPSTAKES

Berger's team, photo by Donna Quante, from the Carrie McLain museum in Nome.

1983 Sweepstakes Queen Caroline Reeder and Champion Rick Swenson. Photo Jan DeNapoli from Carrie McLain Museum.

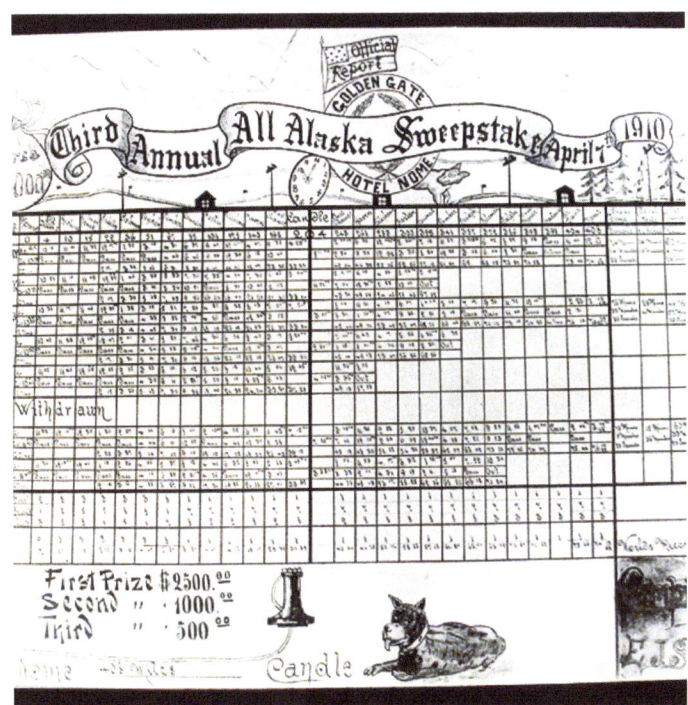

1912 All Alaska Sweepstakes leaderboard. Photo by Jan DeNapoli.

All Alaska Sweepstakes crowd on Front Street at the fourth race in 1911.

An Early Account of the All Alaska Sweepstakes
excerpted from *The Land of Tomorrow*, by William B. Stephenson, Jr.
former U.S. Commissioner at St. Michael, Alaska (©1919, George H. Doran Company, NY)

William B. Stephenson, former United States Commissioner at St. Michael, captioned this photo:
"Coming into St. Michael with our thirty-three-dog team after going out to meet the mail carrier."

The Beginning

Nothing in the history of the country has been of more value to Alaska than the Dog Derby, the "All-Alaska Sweepstakes," as the dog races are called.

Albert Fink, an attorney at Nome, one day overheard a bet between two men as to the speed of their respective dog teams. As he owned some fine dogs himself, he conceived the idea of having a real Derby, matching the teams for the love of the sport itself. Calling together all the dog lovers and dog owners of the community, he put the suggestion before them. The result was the organization of the Nome Kennel Club, a society the purpose of which was to foster the races. The latter were to be known as the "All-Alaska Sweepstakes," and as such the races have been known ever since. The club was organized and conducted just as jockey clubs are. Rules and regulations were drawn up, officers elected, and a purse of fifteen thousand dollars collected for the first race.

Some one has ventured the opinion that nothing on earth could ever have made the city of Nome except the very thing that did make it,—the discovery of gold in the sand on the beach! Be that as it may, it is safe to say that since that discovery nothing has ever equaled the interest it created until the first dog race was held in 1908.

Men talked of nothing else. On the day of the race the stores, banks and offices were deserted and it is a fact that the District Court was forced to adjourn. Witnesses, jurors and attorneys failed to appear. All went to the races. Thousands of dollars were wagered on the dogs, thousands more on the men who drove them. It was a day of great excitement and enthusiasm.

The First Race

The course was from Nome, on Bering Sea, across Seward Peninsula to Candle and back,—a distance of four hundred and ten miles. The first race was a great event. One of the conditions was that the whole team must return to the starting-point. The weather was most severe and some of the dogs froze to death. It is no uncommon sight in Alaska to see an intrepid driver, in harness himself, helping to bring back in the sled the disabled dogs which have become incapacitated by accident or sickness. The man who loses a dog is out of the race, no matter what the cause of the loss may be. The rules provide, however, that after being certified at Candle, the turning-point, the dog does not necessarily have to be driven back. But the whole team must return.

The winning team of the first race were Malamuts owned by Albert Fink, driven by John Hegness. They made the distance in a hundred and nineteen hours, fifteen minutes and twenty-two seconds. The winning team was closely followed by one driven by the now-famous "Scotty" Allen and which made the course in a hundred and twenty hours, seven minutes and fifty-two seconds. Three hours elapsed before the third team came in.

The small margin of time between the first and second teams made the race, which took days to finish, of unusual interest. There was great uncertainty almost up to the last moment. But the race was regarded as a success and the event became a fixture. Heretofore, while there had been much discussion as to the breeding of racing dogs, it had been largely theoretical. Now men who owned dogs began to put their minds on it seriously.

The purse of fifteen thousand dollars collected for the first race was awarded in three prizes. Ten thousand went to the winner, three thousand to the second and two thousand to the third team. It was supposed when the amount was collected that it would be amply sufficient to tempt dog owners to become fanciers and to induce the importation and breeding of faster and better dogs. But the sum was found to be inadequate. The total purse fell far short of the amount necessary to assemble, feed, train and condition a team.

The Following Years

The following year there were numerous entries for the second race. And they were not confined to wealthy dog owners, by any means. Miners, fur traders, mail carriers, to say nothing of the first delegate to Congress, entered the contest. This time "Scotty" Allen came in for his own. He drove his team himself and lowered the time to eighty-two hours, two minutes and forty-two seconds,—thirty-seven hours less than the time the first race had consumed.

Perhaps the most interesting personage in connection with the early dog racing in Alaska is Fox Ramsey. He is an Englishman, the brother of Lord Dalhousie. He was what is commonly known as a Cheechaco,—in other words, a tenderfoot. He was unused to the ways of the trail, and what he did not know about handling dogs would fill a book. But he was a good sport. So he entered his team of Malamuts in the second race and drove them himself. He took any amount of chaff from the local drivers and the amusement of the latter was certainly justified. Several weeks after the race was over Ramsey drove up to the finishing post and with the utmost good humor notified the judges that his team had arrived!

Fox Maule Ramsey

The old saying, however, that "he who laughs last laughs best" is peculiarly applicable to Fox Ramsey. He chartered a schooner bound for Siberia. When he returned, as some one has already recorded, "Siberian huskies howled from every port hole." The crowd which had found so much merriment in his racing team of the previous year laughed louder than ever. They took not the slightest interest in the training of his dogs. Ramsey kept his own counsel. When the time came he entered the race. Then came Ramsey's turn to laugh. He took both first and second money! Not only that, he broke the record. The new one was astonishing. He covered the course in seventy-four hours, fourteen minutes and twenty-two seconds.

The good Alaskans, as always, showed the right spirit. Their amusement changed to admiration. All existing theories as to the best breeds for racing had been completely upset. Ramsey is now at the front "somewhere in France" fighting for his country—and ours! Here's to him!

Famous Racing Dogs

It has often happened that dogs the fame of which has spread not only over Alaska but over all the world have developed from the second string. One such was Baldy of Nome, the hero of a book written by his owner, Mrs. C. E. Darling, commonly known as "The Darling of the Dogs." Baldy is old now, —a pensioner. He lives in ease and luxury at the California estate of his mistress. His story is interesting. He was rejected at first as being not of sufficient caliber for the first team. Whether the rejection spurred him to renewed effort I do not know. But he proceeded to prove his worth. He won his way from wheel of the second team to leader of the first team. Baldy occupies a warm spot in every Alaskan heart. He worked up from the ranks,—a "self-made" dog, so to speak, and proved his courage, his sagacity, his strength, and his endurance. One of the most interesting things about him is that he now possesses the largest service flag of any one of my acquaintance. Twenty-eight of his sons and grandsons went to the Vosges to "do their bit," and Baldy now wears the Croix de Guerre bestowed upon them by the French government!

Of the now-famous dogs of the Derby mention must be made of Dubby. He was the first "loose" leader ever developed in Alaska and the best. He was almost human in intelligence. He ran free from the tow line. He would take his place proudly at the head of his team, with no restraint of tow or leash, observing the spoken commands with instant obedience. From his position of authority at the head of the team, by incessant yelping and playful antics, he would encourage the others, and woe to any one of them that proved the laggard! Dubby promptly punished him. He would run back, bark and then nip him until the offender was only too glad to return to duty and resume gait. Other dogs which have won fame in the Derby are (1) Jack McMillan, a leader belonging to Albert Fink; (2) Rex, a pacer; (3) The Blatchford Blues, two thoroughbred Llewellyn setters, wonderful both as to speed and intelligence; (4) Kalma, a beautiful, white-eyed, black-coated Siberian who has proved the most lasting campaigner of them all. ~•~

ALL ALASKA SWEEPSTAKES

"King of the Alaskan Trail"

Leonhard Seppala's contributions to the All Alaska Sweepstakes, to dog mushing, and to the development of the Siberian Husky cannot be overstated. In *The World of Sled Dogs*, author Lorna Coppinger wrote ten years after Seppala's death in 1967, "No dog driver has the status, the reknown, the respect of his colleagues as does Leonhard Seppala."

In his autobiography, *Seppala: Alaskan Dog Driver*, Leonhard Seppala writes of standing around the Board of Trade Saloon in Nome, "glancing at Scotty Allan, Fay Dalzene, and John Johnson, and I felt greatly honored if I could speak with them. I thought they were wonderful men and admired their achievements greatly. Little did I think that the day would come when I should be battling my way on the Sweepstakes trail against them! When they came in they would look frostbitten and worn out after the storms and cold they had encountered on the trail, and I envied them their experiences."

Seppala's telling of his second Sweepstakes race is a riveting account, and among the most engaging sections are his encounters with champion dog driver Scotty Allan.

Left: Seppala and Togo. Below: Fritz, one of Seppala's leaders on the 1925 Serum Run. Photos by Donna Quante, Carrie McLain museum, Nome.

Seppala plays a cat-and-mouse game with Scotty Allan, explaining that "Scotty was known for his cunning in dog races, and it was commonly believed that he won his races as much by talking the other fellow out of it as anything else."

Seppala did his best to convince Allan that he was no challenge to his bid for the win, and let Allan tell him that he stood a good chance of coming in second. When he was sure Allan was out of sight Seppala urged a little more speed from his team. At the Boston checkpoint the two dog drivers exchanged pleasantries and Allan told Seppala he didn't have to rush to get second place, and as Seppala pulled out he "got a glimpse of Scotty in the window checking up on the condition of my team."

Seppala's dogs were slow to get started, "dragging along and to all appearances were pretty tired and not able to go many miles more; but I was banking on the Siberian traits I knew so well."

Seppala delighted in describing his victorious finish: "Tired as I was, it gave me a thrill which made me forget my fatigue to hear the cannon, and the whistles in Nome from the power plant and the fire stations shrieking their blare of welcome. Great numbers of people were strung along the trail to see the finish, and they shouted their encouragement and approval as I went by. Somehow, I was no longer tired, only glad it was over."

Leonhard Seppala's reputation was created by his victories in the All Alaska Sweepstakes, but the intrepid musher went on to play a pivotal role in the 1925 serum run to Nome, when his famous racing leader, Togo, led Seppala's team through a blinding blizzard and across the treacherous frozen Norton Sound.

Seppala is considered the father of the SIberian Husky, which was accepted as a registered breed by the American Kennel Club in 1930.

Leonhard Seppala often said Togo was his favorite sled dog; named for a Japanese admiral, the tough little Siberian co-led Seppala's team in the 1925 Serum Run with his half-brother, Fritz.

"TOGO"- L. SEPPALA'S LEADER - HERO OF NOME SERUM RACE

Race Marshall and Lead Judge Al Crane, left, discusses details with Race Director Dr. Phil Schobert, center, and Nome Kennel Club historian and Sweepstakes volunteer Howard Farley, right. Photo: Jan DeNapoli.

The Nome Kennel Club, All Alaska Sweepstakes, and 1925 Serum Run

In his classic history of the Nome Kennel Club, written around 1990, Howard Farley gave a good synopsis of what went on in the early years of the race:

"The All Alaska Sweepstakes got its start in 1908. The first race was a very slow race. It was run in about 100 hours, perhaps a little more. The contestants were basically freighting - type teams, which is why the times were slower. In 1909 they decreased the time just a little bit. The record which still stands today, eighty years later, was set in 1910 by teams brought over from the Siberian side. They were Siberian huskies, dogs brought over by Fox Maule Ramsay. He entered three teams in the 1910 All Alaska Sweepstakes and he took the number one position with a man driving for him who was called Iron Man Johnson. That record of 74 hours and some odd minutes stands to this date. Fox Maule Ramsay also took third place at that race with a team of those Siberians that he was driving himself.

"Down through the years, until 1918, the All Alaska Sweepstakes continued with great mushers like Scotty Allan and Leonard Seppala trying, trying and trying to break that record of Iron Man Johnson's. Leonard Seppala was to win the race three times and Scotty Allan was to win it three times, but in all their trying they could not best the record of Iron Man Johnson.

"The Nome Kennel Club carried on its races until after World War One was over in about 1918 and then interest in racing around the Nome area fell off. In 1925 word went out over the wireless from Nome that Nome had some cases of diphteria. At that time Nome was locked into winter and there was no transportation available except dog teams. Airplanes were around at that time but the closest ones were in Fairbanks and they had been put away. So the word went out for serum. Of course the press on the Outside picked this up and this became one of the most heroic and famous epics of all time. The serum was found in Anchorage and it was transported on the Alaska Railroad up to Nenana and from there it was picked up by a series of dog mushers, twenty in all, and it was brought to Nome in 129.5 hours. This is a record that I believe has not been broken to this day.

"Racing continued in Nome. There were minor races held during the time from the serum run up until World War Two. These were shorter races. There were no more All Alaska Sweepstakes races. Racing had moved into the Fairbanks area in those days as well as expanding back East. One of the prime reasons for racing falling off in the Nome area was that gold mining had diminished after World War One and there was not much gold mining until the huge dredges took over in the Nome area. As time went by, there was less and less need for the large teams. Many of the dog teams that Leonhard Seppala and other mushers ran in the old days were owned by the mining companies. They were used for drayage purposes, for hauling freight back and forth to their operations. The mail drivers hauled mail up and down the coast until 1962 when the final dog driver retired for St. Lawrence Island. Over the years, dogs have been a very important part of Nome and its history, both in mining and in dog racing."

This recounting of the Nome Kennel Club history is edited from Howard Farley's original telling. The unedited version can be found at the Nome Kennel Club and All Alaska Sweepstakes web sites.

Below: Leonhard Seppala with Togo. "He has won more races than any dog in Alaska…"

ALL ALASKA SWEEPSTAKES

1983 All Alaska Sweepstakes champion Rick Swenson, left, with his long-time kennel partner Sonny Lindner, at the 2008 All Alaska Sweepstakes. The two mushers combined the best dogs from their respective kennels in both races, taking turns driving the team.

The 1983 Race - The 75th Anniversary

The Special Diamond Anniversary running of the All Alaska Sweepstakes was once again staged by the Nome Kennel Club and followed a course from Nome to Candle and back, also requiring the mushers to finish with all the same dogs with which they started the race. The winner-take-all purse was $25,000, and a silver replica of Leonhard Seppala's trophy. Special bronze belt buckles and green and gold patches were created for the mushers, and the race budget, raised during ten years of planning for the anniversary race, was a respectable $40,000.

Almost two dozen dog drivers entered the 75th running, including Eureka musher, trapper and gold prospector Rick Swenson, who had won the famous Iditarod Trail Sled Dog Race four times, and had run and placed within the top ten in every Iditarod since 1976.

Rick won the 1983 race in 84 hours, 42 minutes, the sixth fastest time in Sweepstakes history, with his by-then famous leader Andy as part of the team. At the top of his game in 1983, when races between him and Susan Butcher were rapidly becoming the stuff of legends, and when a one second loss to 1983 Iditarod Champion Dick Mackey vaulted them both into Iditarod history, Rick went on to become the only five time winner of the Iditarod, a record which still stood in 2010, when he entered his 33rd Iditarod, and had gained him the well-deserved title "King of the Iditarod."

ALL ALASKA SWEEPSTAKES

Rick Swenson's famous leader Andy was the son of Nugget, who Rick purchased from Joe Redington Sr. shortly after he arrived in Alaska from Minnesota in 1973. Andy's sire was Chief, a dog of unknown lineage owned by Ron Tucker. Nugget was also the mother of OB, or Old Buddy, Andy's half brother and his partner in lead and in life until OB passed away in 1991. Andy died in 1993 at the age of 18.

Andy led Rick to victory in four of his five Iditarod wins, the 1983 All Alaska Sweepstakes, and, as part of Rick Swenson's partner Sonny Lindner's team, the tough little husky was also in the inaugural running of the 1,000 mile Yukon Quest in 1984.

Rick called Andy his "secret weapon," because he didn't like to let other teams be ahead of him in a race, and his enthusiasm for passing other teams would muster Rick's entire team to victory. Rick put his faith and trust in Andy during many races, and said "he never let me down his entire career."

Rick had Andy mounted after his death in 1993, and he is on permanent display at the Iditarod Trail headquarters log cabin, near Wasilla, Alaska, next to Leonhard Seppala's famous Togo.

Left: Jon Van Zyle's 1983 All Alaska Sweepstakes poster. Below: Rick Swenson's intrepid leader, Andy, at the Iditarod Trail museum. Photo by June Price.

ALL ALASKA SWEEPSTAKES WINNERS
The race has only been run 12 times

John Hegness – 1908

Scotty Allan – 1909

John Johnson – 1910

Scotty Allan – 1911

Scotty Allan – 1912

Fay Delzene – 1913

John Johnson – 1914

Leonhard Seppala – 1915, 1916, 1917

Rick Swenson - 1983

Mitch Seavey - 2008

HISTORY OF THE ALL ALASKA SWEEPSTAKES

Excerpted from *The Great Dog Races of Nome - Held Under the Auspices of the Nome Kennel Club Official Souvenir History by Esther Birdsall Darling, President, 1916*

Since out of the far North have always come tales of adventure and achievement, hardship and heroism, it is not strange that out of the far north have come also the records of a sport unequalled in history for excitement, speed and endurance -- the records of the famous Dog Races of Nome.

The winter season here extends from departure of the last boat of the open season late October, to the arrival of the first boat early in June, and during this time the people of Northwestern Alaska are cut off from the rest of the world by a barrier of over a thousand miles of ice and snow; the only direct communication with the "Outside" being by weekly Government Dog Team mails, and Wireless Telegraph System.

The men and women of this shut-in community, unusually active mentally and physically as is always the case in any frontier civilization, need an outlet for their superabundant energy in some diversion that is characteristic of their surroundings--for many pleasures are geographically impossible. The diversion they have found in these thrilling contests over the snow-swept wastes of Seward Peninsula.

In this country where dogs have always been an indispensable factor in the work of discovery and settlement, it is hardly surprising that they should be, as well, an indispensable factor in the most popular and representative sport: and it was because of a desire to make this sport a recognized part of the life of the community that the Nome Kennel Club was organized in 1908 with Albert Fink as its first President.

From the very beginning there was much enthusiasm, and generous purses have been offered that have ranged from ten to three thousand dollars, according to the financial conditions prevailing, not only in Alaska, but generally-for many contributions come from liberal friends "Outside."

It was early seen that not only would the races furnish much of the winter entertainment, but that there would also be a consistent effort on the part of the dog owners and dog drivers to improve the breed of sled dogs, which up to this time had been but little considered; an effort to instill into all dog users an intelligent understanding of the accepted fact that care and kindness to their dogs bring the quickest and surest returns from all standpoints. This has resulted in the development of such a high standard for dogs that not alone is their worth acknowledged throughout Alaska, but their supremacy is conceded the world over.

When Amundsen contemplated making a dash to the North Pole, it was to Nome that he wrote for dogs; and while he subsequently gave up the voyage, the dogs selected for him were afterwards used by Leonhard Seppala in a team which twice won the All Alaska Sweepstakes, and the Ruby Derby.

Vilhjalmur Stefansson, too, turned to Nome for dogs when he went at the head of a Canadian Expedition to search for unknown lands and chart unknown waters in the ice floes of the Arctic; and the dogs which "Scotty" Allan bought for that intrepid explorer have been of untold assistance in his great achievements.

ALL ALASKA SWEEPSTAKES

Leonhard Seppala and his Siberian huskies. Photo by Jan DeNapoli at the Carrie McLain Museum, Nome.

ALL ALASKA SWEEPSTAKES

"Between the first and tenth of April the grand climax of the winter series was held in the Alaskan Sweepstakes. This compelled drivers to train all winter long.

"Financially, the race was as big an event in Alaska as the Kentucky Derby is to the racing world. The betting was always very heavy. Sometimes there was as much as one hundred and thirty hundred thousand dollars on the books, with hundreds of side bets for lesser amounts. The books never closed until the first team was home, because there was always a chance, through accident, for the leader to be passed right up to the very end. All the saloons had betting boards, but the principal one was at the headquarters of the race, and the Board of Trade Saloon on Front Street. Of course practically all bets were in gold dust, which was still the chief medium of exchange."
A.A. ("Scotty") Allan, in Gold, Men and Dogs (G.P. Putnam's Sons, 1931)

Gold All Alaska Sweepstakes coin inside an old leatheer sled dog collar, in a display at the Carrie McLain Museum, Nome. Photo by Jan DeNapoli.

ALL ALASKA SWEEPSTAKES

Chapter Two: The Preliminaries

On March 26th, 2008, Nome and the dog mushing world will celebrate the 100th Anniversary of the first major long distance sled dog race in the world. With the centennial re-run of the All Alaska Sweepstakes Race—a distance of 408 miles—we will once again experience the excitement of the early history of the gold rush era in Alaska.
    -letter from Dr. Phil Schobert

Jon Van Zyle's 2008 race poster

ALL ALASKA SWEEPSTAKES

Governor's Declaration

WHEREAS, Nome and the dog mushing world will celebrate the 100th Anniversary of the first major long distance sled dog race in the world. With the centennial rerun of the All Alaska Sweepstakes Race, a distance of 408 miles—we will once again experience the excitement of the early history of the gold rush era in Alaska. (plus other Whereases…)

THEREFORE, I, Sarah Palin, Governor of the state of Alaska, do hereby proclaim March 26, 2008, as All Alaska Sweepstakes 100th Anniversary in Alaska, and wish all the mushers and dog teams well as they embark on this historic race.

The Three Lucky Swedes

Standing next to Nome's famous oversized gold pan are life-sized statues of the "Three Lucky Swedes," who discovered gold in Anvil Creek in 1898 and launched the Nome gold rush: Jafet Lindeberg, John Brynteson and Erik Lindblom, who'd initially come to Alaska as reindeer herders in a U.S. government program to introduce Eskimos to reindeer as an alternate food supply. When the program was cancelled the three men went looking for gold - and found it.

Jafet Lindeberg, who had fished with Leonhard Seppala in Sweden, later brought him to Nome and helped him learn the skills of dog driving.

The Burled Arch

Nome's famous burled arch was created by Red Fox (Richard) Olson, the Red Lantern award winner in the second Iditarod in 1974. After the race Red took on a personal quest to give something special back to the Iditarod organizers and participants, and his original double burled arch, logged from near his home in Fairbanks, stood for 25 years. It is now permanently on display in the Nome recreation hall, where Iditarod and Sweepstakes banquets are held.

The current burled arch, like its much-loved predecessor, greets every musher arriving in Nome.

"Rollicking, careless, golden Nome!"

"When they hit the trail again it was twilight… Past Port Safety they sped in the dusk; past Cape Nome in the dark; past the lighted barracks of the Fort. Then far up the dim coast the silver glow of Nome with the electric cross flashing out a welcome from the church steeple.

"Little, low-lying, ugly Nome! At the sight of it Wally burst into expressions of affection and delight. He was home--home after fifteen hundred miles across frozen Alaska! Home in rollicking, careless, golden Nome!"

-from *The Trail Eater*, by Barrett Willoughby, 1929

ALL ALASKA SWEEPSTAKES

At the corner of Front Street and Bering Street in Nome.

Leonhard Seppala lived in this cabin while in Nome.

Summertime aerial view of Nome and the Bering Sea.

The view across Front Street to the frozen Bering Sea.

ALL ALASKA SWEEPSTAKES

All Alaska Sweepstakes Executive Director & Assistant Director

Dr. Phil and Lisa Schobert, Executive Director and Assistant Director, with their daughter Katie Schobert, a Sweepstakes Queen contestant. In a letter announcing the race they wrote, "Some of you gave your talents-and your hearts-to bring sled dog racing back to center stage in the sporting world. In this, we are all family, and we invite you to come to Nome, to the party, to a reunion with old friends, and to make this a celebration to remember!" Photo: Jan DeNapoli.

All Alaska Sweepstakes Judges

In back, from left to right: Nels Alexie from the Kuskokwim 300 Sled Dog Race, Mark Nordman from the Iditarod Trail Sled Dog Race, and Mike McCowan from the Yukon Quest and North American races. In front, Al Crane, lead judge, and Joe May, a past Iditarod race champion, who will act as an alternate race judge. Not shown: Al Marple from the Copper Basin; Chuck Schaffer from the Kobuk 440; and Jerry Tokar from the Fur Rondezvous. Photo: Jan DeNapoli.

ALL ALASKA SWEEPSTAKES

All Alaska Sweepstakes Pilots

Trail Air Transportation Coordinator Stan Morgan of Nome (in front, left), Jay Wieler (right), Simon Kineen, Doug Doherty and Larry Eggart (back row, left to right). Any modern distance sled dog race depends on the skills and experience of pilots who volunteer their time, equipment, and untold quantities of patience, and the Sweepstakes is no exception. Flying through some of the worst weather on earth, these brave pilots transport supplies, dogs, and people along the trails, although it has been written that some pilots believe sled dog races are staged merely to provide the opportunity to sharpen their winter flying skills. Photo: Jan DeNapoli.

All Alaska Sweepstakes Veterinarian Team

The All Alaska Sweepstakes race veterinary team: Dr. Denise Albert (Lead Vet), from Denali, Alaska, and the Trail Veternarians (not all pictured here: Dennis Griffin, Wausau, Wisconsin; Tex Coady, Henderson, Nevada; Susan Whiton, Willow, Alaska; Caroline Griffitts, Loveland, Colorado; Paul Pifer, Sylvania, Ohio; and Turner Lewis, Wakefield, Massachusetts. A note to the mushers read: "All of the vets recruited are veterans on the trail. They have many years of experience on numerous distance races... These names and faces should inspire confidence and be familiar to you all from working with them in the past." Photo: Jan DeNapoli.

ALL ALASKA SWEEPSTAKES

Dr. Phil and Lisa Schobert

H. Connor Thomas

Jeff King

Mitch Seavey

ALL ALASKA SWEEPSTAKES

Lance Mackey

Fred Moe Napoka

Ed Iten

Aaron Burmeister

ALL ALASKA SWEEPSTAKES

The All Alaska Sweepstakes Queen

At the Musher's meeting and bib drawing, 1983 All Alaska Sweepstakes Queen, Caroline Reader, crowned lifelong Nome resident Janice Doherty as the 2008 All Alaska Sweepstakes Queen with a unique and beautiful sealskin crown. Queen Caroline later donated her own royal robe and crown to the Carrie McLain museum for future generations to enjoy.

The Queen's duties include officially starting all dog teams at the beginning of the race, and greeting the teams on their return. The Queen's Purse was given as prize money for the second place finisher. Janice's grandfather, Robert Snyder, raised his family in Candle, Alaska and moved to Nome by dogteam in 1924. Among Janice's many interests, she has always been involved in photography, writing, geology, camping, fly fishing, and traveling. She also helps her daughter, Chrystiene, with her own team of 22 dogs. Janice has her own Cessna 170-B and is working on her private pilot's license.

Left: Queen Caroline Reader crowns Queen Janice Doherty.
Below: Queen Janice, left, poses with musher Ed Iten and runner-up Tammy Payghutqaq Gologergen.

ALL ALASKA SWEEPSTAKES

In addition to her sealskin crown with beadworked huskies, Janice wore a parka and a traditional native kuspuk in colors with special meanings: brown for the surrounding tundra, blue for the arctic sky, pink for the flowering fireweed, and yellow for the nuggets of gold found in area streams. The trim also signifies the trail her grandfather followed when he moved his family from Candle to Nome.

"Presently the merry jingle of bells, and loud shouts, announced the arrival of the Royal Sled. Covered with magnificent wolf robes... The Queen of the North dashed up to the Royal Box... in one hand she carried a quaintly carved scepter of ivory, made from a huge walrus tusk, and in the other the American flag at whose dip would begin once more the struggle for supremacy of the trail." -Esther Birdsall Darling, Baldy of Nome

Right: 2008 Sweepstakes Queen Janice Doherty. Photo: Jan DeNapoli. Below: Queen Janice Doherty and members of her court, Tammy Payghutqaq Gologergen, Meredith Ahmasuk, Dana Sherman, Dora Mae Hughes, and Katie Schobert, Photo by Sue Steinacher.

ALL ALASKA SWEEPSTAKES

Honorary Bib #1 Pete MacManus' grandsons, Peter MacManus and Jayson Russell, honored the memory of their grandfather by driving the first team out of the chute with bib #1. Pete MacManus ran the Iditarod in 1977 and 1978, finishing in 13th place in both races. In 1977 he won the prized Rookie of the Year award, given to the musher who places the best among those finishing their first Iditarod.

#13 Mike Santos, Cantwell Mike Santos wrote: "When I drove through Broad Pass and the Alaska Range I knew I had found my place. About two years ago the Sweepstakes came up in a conversation and I just can't get it out of my head. I lie awake at night thinking about the event. All the pros and cons. The hows and whys. That sort of thing. Bottom line... If you've got a dog team you've just gotta be there!"

#7 Hugh Neff, Skagway Hugh Neff, a summer tour operator from southeast Alaska, came to the Sweepstakes with previous experience in the Iditarod, the Yukon Quest, the Kobuk 440 and even sprint racing. He wrote: "Racing for me is a celebration of the Northern lifestyle and our beloved dogs. At heart I am an explorer. The Sweepstakes is an opportunity to flow over unknown horizons."

#9 Kirsten Bey, Nome Kirsten Bey, a lawyer and an experienced musher who had lived in Nome for many years, explained why she was running: "I decided to enter the All Alaska Sweepstakes to be part of history and travel the trail and pretend I am in the 'old days.' Since I live in Nome, I would be very disappointed with myself in a few years if I let this opportunity go by."

ALL ALASKA SWEEPSTAKES

#10 Jeff King, Denali Park Jeff King, who owns a kennel near Denali National Park, wrote in his biographical sketch that he came to Alaska in 1975 "for adventure," and as a four time champion of the Iditarod, he found it. Jeff listed his occupation as 'Dog musher,' and in response to the question of why he'd signed up for the All Alaska Sweepstakes he wrote a single word: "History!"

#11 Jeff Darling, Nome Jeff Darling of Nome, no relation to the author Esther Birdsall Darling of "Baldy of Nome" fame, wrote on his entry form for the All Alaska Sweepstakes: "I enjoy life and the Alaskan wilderness. I enjoy animals and love their companionship. My team is comprised of three year olds and yearlings from the same mother. Two litters of nine and a couple from the pound."

#8 Cari Miller, Nome Cari Miller listed her home as Tripple Creek, Nome, and the mother of eight wrote under 'list your racing experience,' "A person has to start somewhere."
  Cari also wrote that her son Michael had gotten her interested in mushing, and "My dogs are not only my teammates but my friends. We are entering upon this journey together and we will finish together."

#4 Jim Lanier, Chugiak Musher and physician Jim Lanier came to Alaska in 1967, and he was the only musher in the 2008 race who had also raced in the 75th Anniversary running in 1983, when he won the Red Lantern as the last musher to cross the finish line. A veteran of many races since then, including 11 Iditarod finishes, Jim stated that he "wouldn't be the Red Lantern this time."

ALL ALASKA SWEEPSTAKES

1983 ALL ALASKA SWEEPSTAKES QUEEN CAROLINE READER

2008 ALL ALASKA SWEEPSTAKES QUEEN JANICE DOHERTY

ALL ALASKA SWEEPSTAKES

Jon and Jona Zan Zyle

Jon Van Zyle's beautiful All Alaska Sweepstakes posters became a premier prize for all to take home from the race.

Checkpoint Supplies

Supplies for the checkpoints awaiting transportation to the points along the trail where mushers will check in.

Dog Care

Tamara Reynolds, partner and hander for musher Hugh Neff, massages one of the dogs' shoulders in the dogyard.

The Nome Follies

The Nome Follies brought a wonderful fun-filled evening of music, dancing, drama, oration, history, can-can girls!

ALL ALASKA SWEEPSTAKES

The Mini Convention Center

Howard Farley and Lance Mackey hanging out at race central in the Nome Mini Convention Center on Front Street.

The Dogs are Ready

Sled dogs ride to the starting area in their transportation box, towed through the streets of Nome behind a snowmachine.

Gas for the Snowmachines

The trail breakers, trail sweeps, and support teams for the mushers all required snowmachines, which required gas.

Dog Lot Manager

Volunteer dog lot manager Dodi Nesbitt makes certain everything flows smoothly for the dogs and the mushers.

47

ALL ALASKA SWEEPSTAKES

Jim Lanier takes his team out of the dogyard on a warm-up run before the big race day. Photo by Jan DeNapoli.

Displaying their checkpoint signboards, volunteers listen to an orientation meeting. Photo by Jan DeNapoli.

ALL ALASKA SWEEPSTAKES

2008 All Alaska Sweepstakes Race Marshal and Lead Judge

The 2008 All Alaska Sweepstakes Race Marshal and Lead Judge, Al Crane, a past president of the Nome Kennel Club and the Iditarod Trail Committee, a top 20 finisher in the Iditarod Trail Sled Dog Race, and the 1983 75th Anniversary All Alaska Sweepstakes Lead Judge. Photo by Mark Hegener.

ALL ALASKA SWEEPSTAKES

Ready to Race

2. Conner Thomas
3. Fred Napoka
4. Jim Lanier
5. Ed Iten
6. Aaron Burmeister
7. Hugh Neff
8. Cari Miller
9. Kirsten Bey
10. Jeff King
11. Jeff Darling
12. Mitch Seavey
13. Mike Santos
14. Ramy Brooks
15. Lance Mackey
16. Cim Smyth
17. Sonny Lindner

ALL ALASKA SWEEPSTAKES

Honorary Team Number One left the starting chute on Front Street for Peter MacManus, a respected dog driver who lived south of Ambler on the upper Kobuk River for several years, where he built a home and was raising his family. Peter MacManus was killed in a plane crash while returning from the 1983 All Alaska Sweepstakes race. The honorary team leaving the start chute was driven by his grandsons Peter MacManus and Jayson Russell. Photo by Jan DeNapoli.

ALL ALASKA SWEEPSTAKES

Chapter Three: The Start

"'Gone to the Dogs' read the signs in Nome as schools and most businesses closed for the start of the All Alaska Sweepstakes. People crowded into the narrow streets, many wearing the colors of their favorite team. 'Inside information' and 'straight tips' were eagerly sought and dispensed. Those with a little information or a little money backed certain teams with judiciously-placed bets. A Queen and her court, wrapped in furs, added to the glamour; they were driven in dog sleds, as ceremoniously as possible, to the judges' stand.

"The noise of the dogs was deafening as they barked incessantly, reflecting the excitement around them, and more than ready for the trail. The drivers busied themselves nervously around their teams, checking again the harnesses, the lines, the long sleds. Food for men and dogs had been distributed at the relay stations along the route, so sleds were loaded with only those necessities for the trail: boots and covering skins for the dogs, a windbreaker and water boots for the driver, and perhaps a small packet of food in case of emergency."

~from The World of Sled Dogs, by Lorna Coppinger (Howell Book House, 1977)

Jim Lanier's team, photo by Jan DeNapoli

ALL ALASKA SWEEPSTAKES

2. H. Connor Thomas moved to Nome in 1978 to work as a volunteer attorney with the federal VISTA program. He began mushing in 1981 and his experience included Nome to Council, Nome to Kotzebue, the Iditarod, the Yukon Quest, the Kuskokwin 300 and more...

Connor was a checker during the 1983 race, at the First Chance Creek checkpoint. He wrote, "I want to run this race because I do not think I will be in a position to run the next race in 2033. I want to thank my sponsors, Kirsten Bey and her brother, Hawker Bey (deceased)."

3. Fred Moe Napoka, a second-generation musher, wrote, "Tuluksak School is the only school in the country that has a dog-sled team as part of our school curriculum." A lifelong resident of "a small place just outside of Tuluksak," Moe - as he's known - had run local Kusko village races and had coached students to run the Bogus Creek 150 and the Junior Iditarod. The original plan of Tuluksak principal Mariah Thomas Wolf had been for a student to run the team, but when the state testing schedule ruled out that option, Moe and a team of Tuluksak students - Crim, Leroy, and Nicholai - took over and readied the Tukulsak team.

4, Jim Lanier's all-white team of huskies has raced across Alaska for four decades, including a dozen Iditarod races with never a scratch. He said collecting white dogs started accidently 15 years ago when he bred two white dogs which produced a large litter. "I thought it would be fun to run an all white team," he explained. "So I either got white dogs or bred white. That's who we are."

Col. Norman Vaughn is credited with naming Lanier's Northern Whites Kennel. For the Sweepstakes race Lanier's team included a black stand-in, which led Lance Mackey to comment that Jim's team looked "like a moving target!"

5. Ed Iten wrote that he was born in Alaska but raised in Minnesota, returning to Alaska in 1973. A member of the Kotzebue Dog Mushers Association, Ed described his mushing experience as "a steady diet of mid and long distance, local 120 and 220 and 440, Kusko 300 and the Iditarod." Often in the top ten, Ed placed second in the 2005 Iditarod.

Only a couple of weeks before the Sweepstakes, Ed had passed under Nome's burled arch in 17th place in the Iditarod, winning the prestigious Leonhard Seppala Humanitarian Award, which recognizes the musher who provides the best care for his dogs during the race.

ALL ALASKA SWEEPSTAKES

6. Aaron Burmeister was born and raised in Nome, listed his home town as Nenana. A graduate of the University of Fairbanks, Aaron got interested in mushing at the tender age of four, when he watched his father, Richard Burmeister, racing in the Iditarod.

Since then Aaron has run the Iditarod eleven times, almost every year since 1994, finishing every race and placing in the top twenty five times.

7. Hugh Neff wrote in his online journal a few weeks before the Sweepstakes race:"...our goal isn't about winning races, it's about living life to the fullest. I don't know if we'll ever come in first place in a race but No One will ever be on a sled for as many miles as this fortunate soul. I have no choice, these dogs are too beautiful to just sit around and be bored in a dogyard. We were born to run, to love, to fly..."

Hugh's partner, Tamara Reynolds, also a musher, would be supplying support at the checkpoints via snowmachine.

8. Cari Miller wrote in her musher profile: "I moved to Alaska from the Los Angeles area of southern California with my husband and four of my children in October, 1998; we took a job as caretakers of a remote fishing lodge in the Bristol Bay area, Alegnagik Island Lodge. We spent the winter on our own island, in the middle of nowhere, in a brand new six bedroom lodge and fell in love with the bush of Alaska. I have not left the state since." She noted that her family - now with eight children - has since lived in Alegnagik, Fairbanks, North Pole, St. Mary's, and now in Nome for the last four years.

9. Kirsten Bey wrote that she came to Alaska to visit with two law school classmates, met Willow musher Vern Halter, and took a job handling for him. She noted that her dogs, while "just a recreational team," were from a variety of sources: "Some can claim 'Granite' (from Susan Butcher's kennel) and 'Andy' (from Rick Swenson's kennel) as great, great grandparents. "I have some who are out of Joe Runyon and Huslia village dogs. I have a dog from the Kotzebue Nordlum line..."

"I've been lucky, they are hard, steady workers. They have always been willing to go - not fast - but then I like to see the scenery."

ALL ALASKA SWEEPSTAKES

10. Jeff King noted on his musher profile that he'd mushed more than 150,000 miles since 1976, leaving California the year before that to take a job as a ranger in Denali National Park.

Jeff has won the Iditarod four times, and won the Yukon Quest in 1989. Other mushing victories include winning the Kuskokwim 300 eight times, The Copper Basin 300 in 1995, the Tustamena 200 in 2000 and 2001, and the International Rocky Mountain Stage Stop Sled Dog Race in 1999.

Known for his inventive nature, Jeff's adaptations include a sit-down sled (with seat belt), and a heated handlebar on his sled.

11. Jeff Darling and his wife Peggy, 15 year residents of Nome, own and operate Nome's Quality Auto Parts, and from that they took their kennel name: Quality Auto Pups. Peggy tossed her hat into the ring as a candidate for the All Alaska Sweepstakes Queen contest, noting the good cause, "to help in providing prize money to the teams that finish the race, albeit not first."

Peggy also wrote that her husband was joining the Centennial Commemorative race "for the historical value and a chance to see some countryside he might not otherwise be able to see by dog team."

12. Mitch Seavey's father, Dan Seavey, was part of the very first Iditarod in 1973, and he triggered a lifelong family love of mushing. Mitch's racing record includes firsts in most Alaskan distance races, including the Iditarod in 2004. In 2001 Mitch, his father, and his son Danny all completed the Iditarod, in a three-generation finish. And that same year his son Tyrell took first place in the Jr. Iditarod.

For the 1995 Iditarod, Mitch hitched up his team at his home in Seward and mushed the entire length of the historic route, the only Alaskan trail in the National Historic Trail System.

13. Mike Santos says his love of adventure dates back to his childhood, when he'd read accounts of the polar explorers getting stranded, watching their ships getting crushed by the ice, and making a heroic dash for land with their sled dogs.

"I always thought those days were long gone, and then Will Steger re-enacted Robert Peary's historic trek to the North Pole, and National Geographic chronicled it on their weekly program, *Explorer*. That was it, I was going to be a polar explorer, then I heard about the Iditarod and my life has never been the same."

ALL ALASKA SWEEPSTAKES

14. Ramy Brooks of Healy was born in Fairbanks and raised in a Yukon River fish camp. He won his first race in the Junior North American Championships at the age of four, and by the time he was fourteen he'd won every class of the race.

Ramy's mother, Roxy Wright, and his grandfather, Gareth Wright, both blazed stellar careers through the Alaskan mushing scene, and Ramy's own impressive record includes a first in the Yukon Quest in 1999, and Iditarod finishes in fourth place (2000), second place in 2002 and 2003, eighth in 2004 and fifth in 2005. His kennel name, Kami, is Japanese for *sacred spirits*.

15. Lance Mackey mushed into history on the back of his dogsled. In 2007 he won the Yukon Quest and the Iditarod with many of the same dogs - a feat which most thought was impossible. He did it again the next year and changed the very perceptions of long distance mushing and what well cared for dogs were capable of achieving.

A lifelong Alaskan and a cancer survivor, Lance hails from a multi-generational sled dog racing family. His father, Dick Mackey, was instrumental in the first Iditarod, and he won by the closest margin in the history of that race in 1978. Lance's brother Rick also won the Iditarod, in 1983.

16. Cim Smyth, a wildland firefighter, says he's been mushing dogs "since I was big enough." Born and raised in Alaska, Cim is the son of Iditarod finisher Lolly Medley, creator of the race's Golden Harness award, and the legendary Bud Smyth, who ran the inaugural Iditarod in 1973.

In 1978 Bud was back, with 35 dogs, and the Iditarod subsequently changed its rules about how many dogs could be in a team.

Cim entered and finished his first Iditarod in 1996, skipped a couple of years, and then finished every year since 2003, improving his time to Nome and increasing his winnings.

17. Sonny Lindner of Fairbanks won the inaugural Yukon Quest in 1984, having taken up sled dog racing in 1977. A frequent Iditarod contender, placing in the top ten five times, Sonny considers finishing any race with a strong, healthy team "a significant achievement."

Once called "a dog musher's dog musher," Sonny built a solid reputation as one of the best trainers and racers. He teamed up with the only five-time Iditarod Champion, Rick Swenson, for the 1983 race, when Swenson drove the team to victory. In the 2008 race, it's Sonny's turn to drive.

2. H. Connor Thomas

3. Fred Moe Napoka

4. Jim Lanier

5. Ed Iten

ALL ALASKA SWEEPSTAKES

6. Aaron Burmeister

7. Hugh Neff

8. Cari Miller

9. Kirsten Bey

ALL ALASKA SWEEPSTAKES

10. Jeff King

11. Jeff Darling

12. Mitch Seavey

13. Mike Santos

14. Ramy Brooks

15. Lance Mackey

16. Cim Smyth

17. Sonny Lindner

ALL ALASKA SWEEPSTAKES

• Bib No. 2. H. Connor Thomas

• Bib No. 3. Fred Moe Napoka

All photos by Jan DeNapoli

ALL ALASKA SWEEPSTAKES

• Bib No. 4. Jim Lanier

• Bib No. 5. Ed Iten

All photos by Jan DeNapoli

ALL ALASKA SWEEPSTAKES

• Bib No. 6. Aaron Burmeister

ALL ALASKA SWEEPSTAKES

• **Bib No. 7. Hugh Neff**

All photos by Jan DeNapoli

ALL ALASKA SWEEPSTAKES

• Bib No. 8. Cari Miller

ALL ALASKA SWEEPSTAKES

• Bib No. 9. Kirsten Bey

All photos by Jan DeNapoli

• Bib No. 10. Jeff King

• Bib No. 11. Jeff Darling

All photos by Jan DeNapoli

ALL ALASKA SWEEPSTAKES

• Bib No. 12 Mitch Seavey

ALL ALASKA SWEEPSTAKES

• Bib No. 13. Mike Santos

All photos by Jan DeNapoli

ALL ALASKA SWEEPSTAKES

• Bib No. 14. Ramy Brooks

ALL ALASKA SWEEPSTAKES

• **Bib No. 15. Lance Mackey**

All photos by Jan DeNapoli

ALL ALASKA SWEEPSTAKES

• Bib 16. Cim Smyth

ALL ALASKA SWEEPSTAKES

• Bib No. 17. Sonny Lindner

All photos by Jan DeNapoli

ALL ALASKA SWEEPSTAKES

The All Alaska Sweepstakes Dogteams

Mark Hegener collected the names of the dogs on on the race teams from the mushers just prior to the start of the race:

Team No. 1. Peter MacManus: King, Yoda, Kiwi, Koa, Patten, Paul, Perum, Knik, Peter, Owen, By

Team No. 2. Connor Thomas: Ali6, Ali, Juneau, Jazz, Cus, AJ, Biscuit, Violet, Frostbite, Ginger, Flanders

Team No. 3. Fred Moe Napoka: Clark, Angus, Harlen, Bug, Lewis, Siv, Eva, Io, Liberty, Iris

Team No. 4. Jim Lanier: Laika, June, Smokey, Bee, February, October, Valentino, Toby, Moppy, Uma, April, Perro

Team No. 5. Ed Iten: Zorro, Rat, Hover, Zane, Viper, Piker, Zippy, Deak, Ulu, Zar, Arrow, Guy

Team No. 6. Aaron Burmeister: Elim, Cadillac, Wade, Ursula, Banshee, Peanut, Attla, Roxy, Lucky, Beagle, Fiat

Team No. 7. Hugh Neff: Flame, Wild Bill, Colby, Scotty, Annie, Maestro, Spencer, Oscar, Nathan, Jackson, Mahousie, Walter, Omen

Team No. 8. Cari Miller: Gussie, Sanchez, Judas, Rudolph, Rattle, Arnie, Jack, Juri, Storm, Dora, Kinko, Kende, Noonan

Team No. 9. Kirsten Bey: Sonny, Coho, Busher, Brother, Rigel, Roger, Betelgeuse, Q, Pippi, Varden, Blizzard

Team No. 10. Jeff King: Berkeley, Bronte, Call, Charles, Deets, Dickens, Dublin, Guiness, Kilarney, Lobben, Solomon, Sussex, UConn

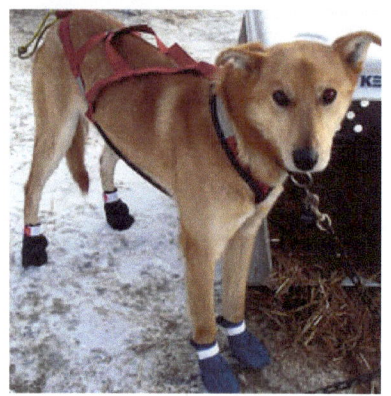

Team No. 11. Jeff Darling: Gunny, Tank, Smedley, Kissy, Gabby, Step, Hazer, Tiny, Price, Mona, Rudy, Sandy

ALL ALASKA SWEEPSTAKES

Team No. 12. Mitch Seavey: Payton, Ditka, Eagle, Dryfus, Hudson, Beetlejuice, Monson, Kirby, Colonel, Hammer

Team No. 13. Mike Santos: Nestor, Phoebe, Inca, Hawkeye, Icarus, Iowa, Indiana, Lethal, Lugnut, Jocker, Lisbon, Knickers, Oezy, Kermit, Nitro, Hook

Team No. 14. Ramy Brooks: Bean, Bishop, Chess, Reece, Marlin, Coke, Windex, Vickers, Sun, Skittles, Nigel, Tiller, Dust

Team No. 15. Lance Mackey: Paulie, Zorro, Curry, Fudge, Battel, Hobo, Boycuz, Hansen, Pimp, Larry, Rapper, Handsome, Rev

Team No. 16. Cim Smyth: Beaver, Squirt, Sid, Brownie, Cactus, Shire, Guy, Thorn, Zeus, Emiua, Harrah, Thor

Team No. 17. Sonny Lindner: Dogs' names not available.

The All Alaska Sweepstakes Queen's Team of Husky Men: Buford Salaffie, Lanka Peacock, Jim Erickson, Stan Morgan, Bruce Tungwenuk, Marlin Sookiyak, Kevin Ahl, Doug Doherty, Rodney Junes, Mike Moore, Daniel Brugliera, Jay Wieler

From *Baldy of Nome*, by Esther Birdsall Darling:

   Matt brought out the long tow-line, and placed it carefully on the floor.
   "Rex and McMillan in the wheel, like we've been usin' 'em, I suppose?" and at a nod he released them.
   "Wheel, Jack; wheel Rex," and they took their accustomed places next to the sled, and remained motionless, yet keenly alert. "Tom and Dick, Harry and Tracy, Irish and Rover"--name after name was called, and each dog stepped into position with joyful alacrity. They were, one and all, sturdy, intelligent, and spirited, with the stamina of their wild forebears, and the devoted nature of those dogs who have for generations been trained to willing service and have been faithful friends to their masters. And then came the expected order: "Baldy in the lead, Matt."

ALL ALASKA SWEEPSTAKES

Judge Mark Nordman from the Iditarod Trail Sled Dog Race. Photo by Jan DeNapoli.

ALL ALASKA SWEEPSTAKES

Judge Nels Alexie from the Kuskokwim 300 Sled Dog Race. Photo by Jan DeNapoli.

ALL ALASKA SWEEPSTAKES

"The cold wind blew fiercely, driving sharp, icy sleep into Baldy's face, but the dog pushed on. Musher Scotty Allan was depending on him. The storm worsened as Baldy and the rest of the team headed out of Spruce Creek. Blinding ice filled the air, and even Scotty couldn't find the trail.

"With darkness approaching, Scotty got off the sled and moved Baldy and Kid into the front positions. Scotty had never chosen Baldy as a leader before. Then Scotty donned snowshoes and tromped out the trail in front of his team. The two lead dogs, harnessed in tandem, followed him up Topkok Hill. Straining with all his might, Baldy pulled the tug line connecting him to the rest of the team and the sled. Finally they descended the hill, through the clouds, with Baldy and Kid leading the team into Topkok, where a warm camp waited at the Timber Roadhouse."
~from Gold Rush Dogs, by Claire Rudolf Murphy and Jane G. Haigh (Alaska Northwest Books, 2001)

Aaron Burmeister's team near Council. Photos on both pages: Jan DeNapoli.

ALL ALASKA SWEEPSTAKES

Chapter Four: The Race

Have you broken trail on snowshoes?
Mushed your huskies up the river.
Dared the unknown, led the way
and clutched the prize?
    ~Robert Service

Lance Mackey near Council

83

ALL ALASKA SWEEPSTAKES

Checkpoints

It's a big, wild, open, empty land... And the practical modes of transportation are snowmachine and airplane. But for all the modern improvements in how people move through it, the land itself has changed but little since the Episcopal archdeacon of the Yukon, Hudson Stuck, drove his dogteam through here in the first few years of the twentieth century. Between 1904 and his death in 1920, the intrepid administrator of the church's affairs traveled the land by dogteam in winter (and utilized the rivers in summer), and he wrote one of the most compelling accounts of winter travel in Alaska, titled *Ten Thousand Miles with a Dog Sled, A Narrative of Winter Travel in Interior Alaska* (New York: Scribners, 1914).

Hudson Stuck minced no words in describing the Seward Peninsula: "A savage, forbidding country, this whole interior of the Seward Peninsula, uninhabited and unfit for habitation; a country of naked rock and bare hillside and desolate, barren valley, without amenities of any kind and cursed with a perpetual icy blast."

Into this unforgiving maw plunged the sixteen teams of the 2008 Centennial Running of the All Alaska Sweepstakes.

Left: Near Council. Below: Bush transportation, Simon Kineen's plane, Stang family snowmachines, on the Niukluk River at Council.

ALL ALASKA SWEEPSTAKES

The volunteers who manned the checkpoints along the trail brought a level of safety, security, and convenience to the teams crossing this harsh land. Many of the checkpoint teams were people who had volunteered 25 years earlier. The checkpoints, in order and with mileages both outbound and inbound:

Nome 0 and 408
Fort Davis 3.4 and 404.5
Hastings 10 and 398
Cape Nome 15 and 393
Safety 22 and 386
Solomon 36 and 372
Topkok 51 and 357
Timber 67 and 341
Council 85 and 323
Boston 108 and 306
Telephone 125 and 283
Haven 140 and 268
First Chance 165 and 243
Gold Run 176 and 232
Candle 204

Right: Timber Checkpoint, by Sue Steinacher.
Below: Checkpoint activity, by Jan DeNapoli

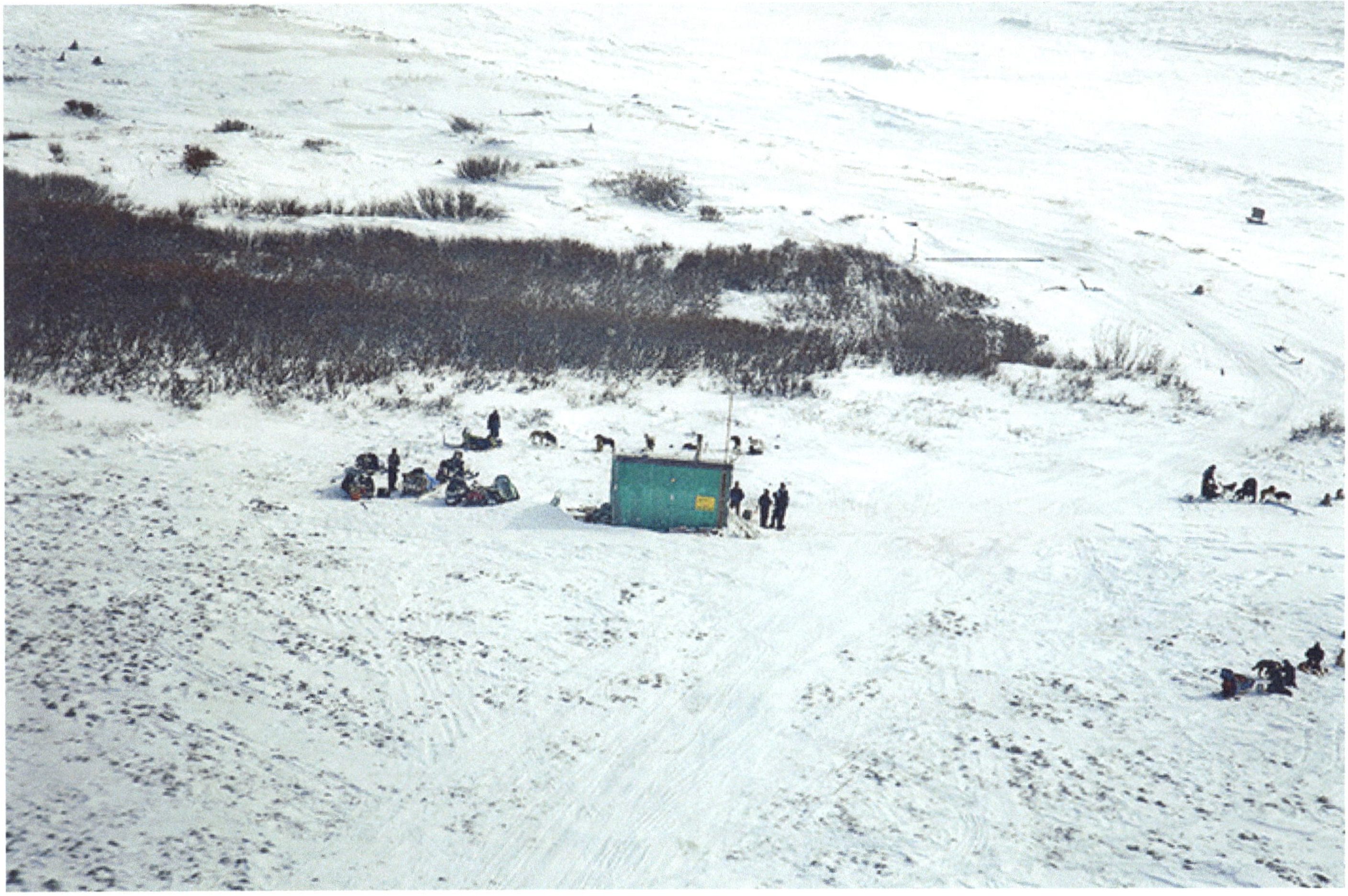

ALL ALASKA SWEEPSTAKES

The old church at Council

A team on the trail near Council

A veterinarian checks over a dog at Council

Popular transportation mode in Council: The Sofa

Council checkpoint, mile 85 outbound, 323 inbound

Drop bags lined up at the Council checkpoint

Council Checkpoint

The checkpoint at Council, mile 85 outbound and mile 323 on the return trip, is a busy place in the summertime, as many Nome residents have homes in the Council area, and there is a gravel road between the two towns. Located on the Niukluk River, Council is the nearest site to Nome which has trees, and reisdents of Nome sometimes travel to Council to cut spruce trees to use as Christmas trees.

Council was founded in 1897 when gold was discovered in nearby Ophir Creek, and by 1898 the area may have had as many as 15,000 inhabitants. The residents around Council left when larger quantities of gold were discovered near Nome around the turn of the century, but they left behind many old buildings and much mining equipment, including a gold dredge. A second, larger dredge is located at 15 Mile Camp on Ophir Creek.

Once part of the Bering land bridge, the Seward Peninsula projects about 200 miles into the Bering Sea between Norton Sound, the Bering Strait, the Chukchi Sea, and Kotzebue Sound, just below the Arctic Circle. The peninsula is 210 miles long and 90 miles wide.

Checkpoint team at Council for the All Alaska Sweepstakes was Dan and Maggie Stang and Al Morton.

Council checkpoint. All photos from Council by Jan DeNapoli.

ALL ALASKA SWEEPSTAKES

A team on the trail. Photo by Jan DeNapoli.

ALL ALASKA SWEEPSTAKES

Trail markers coming into the Council checkpoint. Photo by Jan DeNapoli.

ALL ALASKA SWEEPSTAKES

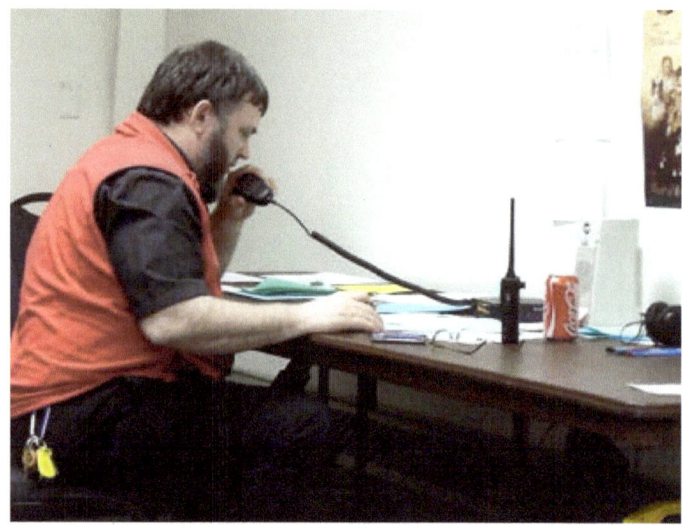

Executive Director Dr. Phil Schobert

Les Brown taking a checkpoint report

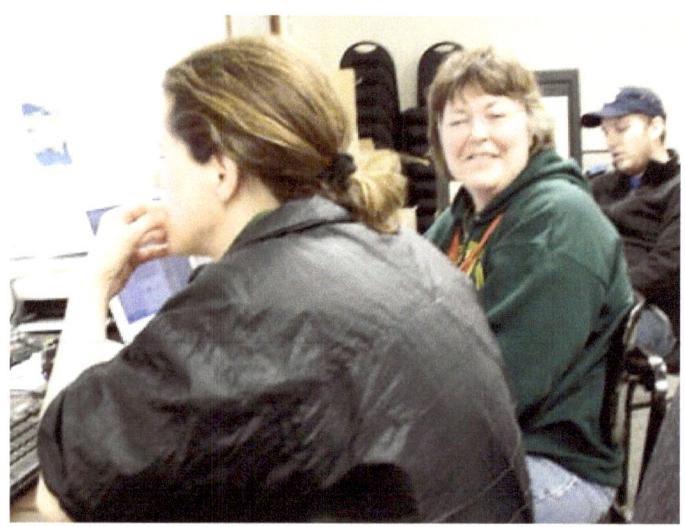

Jodi Bailey, Theresa Daily and Josh Rogers

Jodi Bailey, Johnny Johnson, Mark Hegener

Jodi Bailey, Josh Rogers, Theresa Daily, Kevin Klott

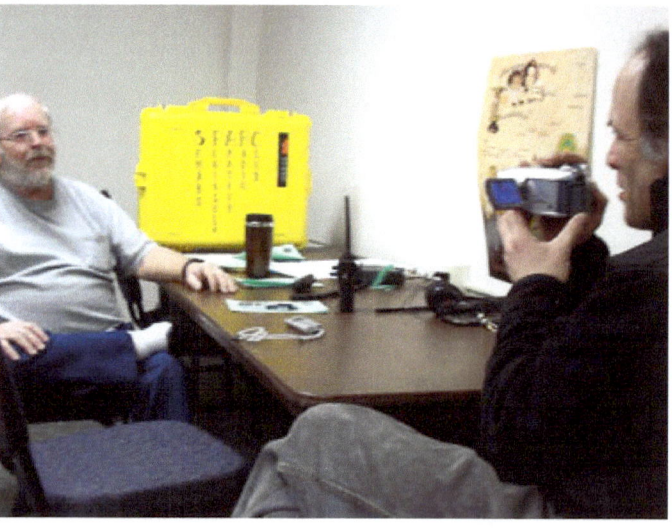

Mark Hegener interviewing Colby Carter, SPARC

ALL ALASKA SWEEPSTAKES

Pilot Simon Kineen

Pilot Jay Wieler makes a preflight check

Many pilots volunteered their time and planes

Drop bags waiting

Supply crews shuffled food, gear, and more

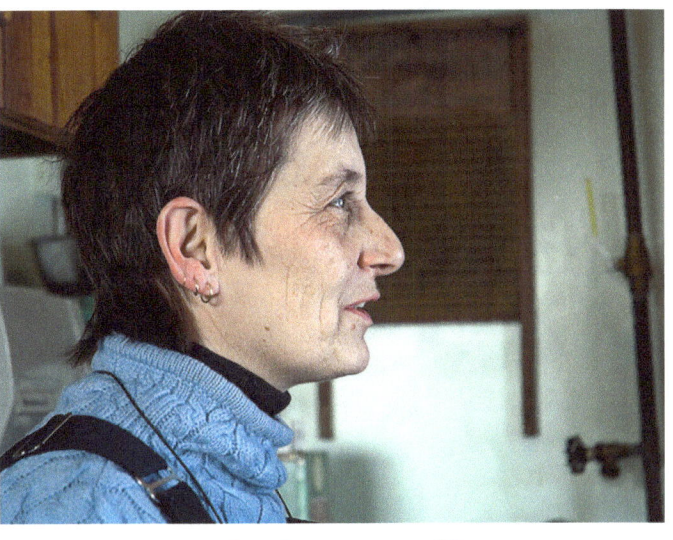
Veterinarian Susan Whiton

ALL ALASKA SWEEPSTAKES

Historic Race Rules

The 2008 All Alaska Sweepstakes adopted the historical version of the rules of the race which were in effect in 1917, which had been adapted from the original rules laid forth in 1908/1909. From the official rules handbook for the 2008 race:

The 1908/1909 version of the rules stated that "Each team entered... consist(ed) of as many dogs as the owner... deem (ed) fit." However, historical photos generally indicate that 16 dogs were the average; thus, in the interests of the welfare of the dogs and to ensure adequate dog care-including the problems of taking care of too many dogs or the obvious problems of including too few-the Nome Kennel Club strongly recommends that mushers consider using the number of dogs that they can adequately care for and the number of dogs that will provide power enough to assure that their trip to Candle and return will be accomplished in a timely and humane manner.

There were no dog drops on the All Alaska Sweepstakes - mushers were expected to return with all their dogs, whether harnessed on the towline or resting in the sled basket. An excerpt from the *Nome Nugget Mining Edition 1908*:

The distance was made four hundred and forty miles in order to force the drivers to nurse their dogs...! To further insure against any cruelty or over taxation of the strength and endurance of the dogs, a very salutary rule was adopted, that each driver must return to the starting point with every dog that he started out with and none others, so that the driver of each team was forced to take the utmost care of each dog in order to comply with the rule."

As for the mushers themselves, it was duly noted in the rules: "Mushers must be prepared with proper cold weather gear. (Seward Peninsula storms are historical and care should be taken for extreme conditions."

Tending to a dog's feet on the trail.

ALL ALASKA SWEEPSTAKES

Jeff King warms up with a cup of coffee

Veterinarian Susan Whiton at the Stang cabin

Council checkpoint

Freight sled at Council

Ed Iten ready to get back on the trail

Lance Mackey takes a break at Council

ALL ALASKA SWEEPSTAKES

A team takes a break from the trail

Jim Lanier's all-white team, with one black dog, which Lance Mackey dubbed 'The Target'

Lance Mackey's teammates Zorro (front) and Fudge, waiting at a checkpoint

ALL ALASKA SWEEPSTAKES

The dogs are checked over carefully while they rest at a checkpoint

Checking the sled for needed repairs or adjustments

Team coming into a checkpoint

ALL ALASKA SWEEPSTAKES

Lance Mackey watching the plane

Mitch Seavey

Mitch Seavey's team moving along the trail

Dinner for a hungry team

Moving smartly down the trail

Makeshift but effective transportation

ALL ALASKA SWEEPSTAKES

On the Niuluk River, near the Council checkpoint

97

The Fairhaven Hospital at Candle, built from salvaged barge timbers. Photo by Joe May.

Halfway Point at Candle

By Thursday, March 27, the three race leaders had reached the halfway point at Candle. Jeff King arrived in Candle at 2:45 p.m.; Lance Mackey arrived just after 3:00 pm, followed closely by Mitch Seavey.

King's run to Candle took 28 hours and 26 minutes, leaving a comfortable 45 hours to make the run back to Nome and still break the race record which had been set by John "Iron Man" Johnson in 1910.

Laura Samuelson, director of the Carrie McClain Memorial Museum, said conditions had been perfect during that 1910 All-Alaska Sweepstakes race. "In 1910 that was the height of the use of this trail, which was a trail that ran about 204 miles to Candle and back to Nome. It was also out to different mining camps so that trail was most likely in peak condition at that time and the conditions were just right."

John "Iron Man" Johnson took advantage of those trails, racing to victory in 74 hours, 14 minutes and 37 seconds with his team of Siberian huskies.

Right and Below: Candle, Alaska. Photos by Joe May.

ALL ALASKA SWEEPSTAKES

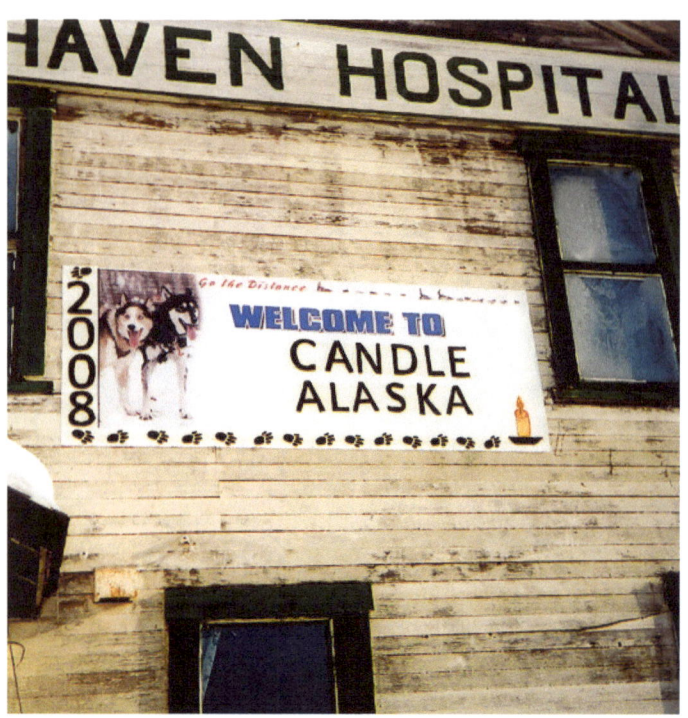

Candle Checkpoint
On northern end of Seward Peninsula

Chuck and Peggy Fagerstrom
Host & Hostess of Candle Checkpoint

"Two Buckland folks who hauled gas from Buckland to Candle and Gold Run and helped where needed..."

"Vic the miner and Larry Eggart and his ski-equipped Maule airplane."

Larry Westlake, Mike Sherman and Joe May.

Marlene Moto of Deering

Larry Eggart's Maule at Candle

Unidentified volunteer with an early leaderboard

ALL ALASKA SWEEPSTAKES

Candle Checkpoint Crew and Visitors
Fagerstrom's "Fairhaven Hospital" in background

Photographer's note from Joe May, April, 2008: "Don't have all the names. Vic "the miner" from Palmer. Mark & Marcia (of the world class caribou ribs) Fairbanks from Kotzebue. Lady in the middle?? (my apology). Mike Sherman (checker) Palmer; Larry Westlake (checker) Kiana; Dorothy Sherman (cook)."

ALL ALASKA SWEEPSTAKES

"Now the big question: Is there enough trail left?"

On the third day of the race Jeff King was still leading, arriving at the Timber checkpoint, 67 miles from the end of the race, at around 1:00 pm, with a three hour lead. Lance Mackey had begun falling behind, while Mitch Seavey had moved up into second place.

KTUU Channel 2 news reporter John Carpenter explained the situation: "On the trails just outside of Council, Friday morning, King had the All-Alaska Sweepstakes lead all to himself.

Meantime, Seavey was resting his team at the checkpoint in Council while Mackey was still several miles on the other side of Council with a team that appeared to be floundering. One of Mackey's wheel dogs, Zorro, appeared to be slowing down the rest of the team and ending Mackey's hopes of winning the centennial running.

"'Well, we've got an issue,' Mackey said. 'I think I'm going to be pretty fortunate to stay right where I'm at, and very content with that. As long as my team looks the way they did coming in here at the finish line, my finishing position is irrelevant.'

"That leaves just two teams competing for the $100,000 purse. Even though King got a three hour jump on Seavey leaving Council, the Seward musher is feeling pretty good about his position.

"'Yeah, I might be winning,' Seavey said. 'So, yeah, that's a good spot. I think I've got the best team. I may not be in the best position, but I might be able to change that.'

"Mackey concurs and he's had pretty good looks at both his competitors.

"'Seavey's team has been moving real nice,' Mackey said. 'I was very, very surprised to see him sitting here when I got here. From watching the times in the last couple of checkpoints, he was definitely gaining on King. If it was me on the sled runners on that team I would not be sitting here, not at all.'

"Now the big question: Is there enough trail left for Seavey's faster team to erase King's three hour lead?

"'I should be moving faster when we leave here so you never know what will happen,' Seavey said."

While King appeared to have a comfortable lead, *Anchorage Daily News* reporter Kevin Klott's headline story in the March 29th newspaper explained what happened next:

"With green northern lights dancing across the sky, Seavey departed Camp Haven on the edge of Death Valley at 2:40 a.m., Friday -- situated in a three-way logjam of former Iditarod champions. Seavey, the 2004 winner, was 43 minutes behind King and 18 minutes ahead of Mackey. Seavey steadily trimmed 38 minutes off King's lead on their way into Solomon. Seavey, 47, was riding on the heels of King as they left Solomon just five minutes apart, leaving Mackey in the dust with only 36 miles left in the 408-mile round-trip race from Nome to Candle."

Left: Volunteers at Candle. Photos by Joe May.

ALL ALASKA SWEEPSTAKES

Mitch Seavey arrived at the finish line in Nome first, at 11:29 pm, ten minutes ahead of second place finisher Jeff King. A large crowd turned out to welcome the 2008 All Alaska Sweepstakes Champion, who said, "I never thought anything could surpass winning the Iditarod, but this a rare event and a pretty nice prize."

Then he thoughtfully added, "It's hard believe, isn't it? It's hard to believe. It's like any dog race, but I can't get my mind wrapped around the whole $100,000 thing."

Mitch Seavey, son of Dan Seavey, who had been one of the Iditarod Trail Sled Dog Race's founding fathers, had broken John "Iron Man" Johnson's 98-year record by coming into Nome in 61 hours, 29 minutes and 41 seconds. Johnson's 1910 time had been 74 hours, 14 minutes, and 17 seconds.

Mitch walked down his team and checked his dogs, then went back and handed his mail caches to the race marshal, posed for a few photos with officials and family and friends, and then rode his sled off to the dog yard at the end of Front Street. It was almost an anticlimactic finish. Jeff King rode into a second place finish ten minutes later, and likewise retired to the dog yard after the formalities.

Two and a half hours later Lance Mackey arrived and, although trail-worn and weary, the reigning Iditarod and Yukon Quest champion accompanied his fans into the nearby Board of Trade Saloon and spent a couple of hours answering questions, posing for photos, telling tales of the trail, and showing once again why he's the perennial crowd favorite in any sled dog race he enters.

Race judge Mark Nordman. Photo by Joe May.

Char Keehn, Ft. Davis checkpoint. Photo: Joe May.

Volunteer. Photo by Joe May.

Safety checkpoint. Photo by Jan DeNapoli.

ALL ALASKA SWEEPSTAKES

Checkpoint Volunteers & Trail Crews

Above: Coat hanging in a checkpoint. Left: Camp Haven, located in Death Valley, 124 miles from the start. Center: Stan and Donna Morgan; Judges Chuck Schaffer, Mike McCowan, and Al Crane; and pilot Jay Weiler, right.

Nome
- Jon & Jona Van Zyle
- Leo Rasmussen
- Howard Farley
- Jo Crane

Fort Davis
- Char Keehn

Hastings
- Jim & Chris Rowe

Cape Nome
- Bonnie Hahn
- Becky Irish
- Pat Hahn

Safety
- Lance & Stephanie Johnson
- Tom Ellanna

Solomon
- Dionne Hartman
- Randy Oles
- Ray Peterson

Topkok
- Lew & Loki Tobin

Timber
- Sue Steinacher
- Glen Pardy

Council
- Dan Stang
- Maggie Stang
- Al Morton

Boston
- Ramon Gandia
- Ken Shapiro

Telephone
- Roger & Amos Thompson

Haven
- Donna Morgan
- Stan Morgan
- Jim Stimple
- Tom Sparks
- Roy Ashenfelter

First Chance
- Charlie Lean
- Tom Vadun
- John Bockman

Gold Run
- Ken Upchurch
- Melissa Ford
- Lester Hadley

ALL ALASKA SWEEPSTAKES

Gold Run (continued)
Fletcher Gregg Jr.
Delbert & Mariah Thomas
Chester Hadley
Eric Morris

Candle
Chuck & Peggy Fagerstrom

Mike & Dorothy Sherman
Larry Westlake
Charlotte Mathias
Bob & Kathy Douglass
Brian Weinard
Beverly Moto
Vic Lawyer III

Trail Crew
Mitch Erikson
Roger & Amos Thompson
Delbert & Mariah Thomas
Phil Prizmont

Ken Upchurch
Lester Hadley
Fletcher Gregg Jr.
Chester Hadley

Glen Pardy and Sue Steinacher at the Timber checkpoint. Photo by Sue Steinacher.

2008 Centennial All Alaska Sweepstakes Champion Mitch Seavey

Mitch Seavey's leaders Payton and Ditka crossed the finish line at 11:29:45 pm, with an elapsed trail time of 61 hours, 29 minutes, and 45 seconds, breaking the record set by John "Iron Man" Johnson in 1910. Finish line checker Leo Rasmussen; the Mayor of Nome, Denise Michaels; Sweepstakes Queen Janice Doherty, and an enthusiastic crowd welcomed the new champion of the Centennial All Alaska Sweepstakes. Photos both pages by Jan DeNapoli.

ALL ALASKA SWEEPSTAKES

Chapter Five: The Finish

"My wife, the Sweepstakes Queen, was the first to reach me, and the crowd went wild with excitement, as always happened when the winner arrived. I was torn from the runners, lifted to the shoulders of the enthusiastic mob, and carried to a little sled drawn by fur-clad young people. Cameras were clicking all around, and, as I was wet with persperation from excitement and some hard work at the end of the trail, the general delay set my teeth chattering.

"Someone brought me a cup of whiskey, and, scarcely knowing what I was doing, I drained every drop of it. I was given a bath and a rub-down, and told those who were looking over my welfare that I would be with them to dance that evening at the celebration given by the Kennel Club.

"I began to get so drowsy I could hardly keep my eyes open, and stopped only long enough to go down to the finish line and greet Scotty. I then returned to my cabin, where with the combination of the whiskey and my general weariness I fell asleep, and it was late on the afternoon of the next day when I again saw daylight."
~Leonhard Seppala, in *Seppala, Alaskan Dog Driver*, by Elizabeth Ricker

109

ALL ALASKA SWEEPSTAKES

Mitch Seavey's leaders, Payton and Ditka, lead his team to the finish line in Nome.

After 400 miles of Alaskan bush, crowds awaiting their arrival are a strange sight.

His mustache coated with frost, Mitch Seavey becomes winner of the 2008 All Alaska Sweepstakes.

Trail-weary, but happy to be the champion, Mitch talks to Jon Van Zyle as Dr. Phil Schobert looks on.

ALL ALASKA SWEEPSTAKES

Jeff King, four-time champion of the Iditarod Trail Sled Dog Race, arrives in second place.

Jeff King arrived at the finish line only ten minutes behind Mitch Seavey.

Lance Mackey's team was hit by a snowmachine near Nome. He poses with his leaders in third place.

Lance with his mother, Kathie Smith, who greeted him at the finish line under the burled arch.

ALL ALASKA SWEEPSTAKES

Teammate Rick Swenson with Sonny Lindner and his partner, musher Kelly Williams.

Sonny Lindner, who finished the race in fourth place, with his daughter Ava.

A very happy Ed Iten of Kotzebue, a musher since 1977, arrives in Nome in fifth place.

Ed Iten chats with Race Marshal and fellow veteran musher Al Crane at the finish line in Nome.

ALL ALASKA SWEEPSTAKES

Jim Lanier's son Jimmy rode the runners with his dad, down Front Street to finish in sixth place.

Jim Lanier sorts out his mail caches as Race Marshal Judge Al Crane looks on.

Negotiating past traffic, Cim Smyth's team enters the finish chute on Front Street.

As Race Marshal Al Crane looks on, Queen Janice welcomes Cim Smyth to Nome in seventh place.

113

Ramy Brooks was greeted by UAA student Dora Mae Hughes and Queen Janice Doherty.

Ramy Brooks smiles at a comment from Race Marshal Al Crane.

Aaron Burmeister finishes ninth with Race Marshal Al Crane jogging alongside.

Aaron Burmeister, who moved from Nome to Nenana in 2002, with his wife Mandy.

Fred Moe Napoka crossed the finish line in tenth place with the Tuluksak School team.

Fred Moe Napoka poses with his leaders from the Tuluksak School team.

Connor Thomas, the eleventh musher to finish, smiles with Sweepstakes Queen Janice Doherty.

Connor Thomas with a leader. Connor was a checker at First Chance Creek checkpoint in 1983.

Cari Miller chats with Race Marshal Al Crane as she comes into Nome in twelfth place.

Cari Miller, who lives near Nome with her family, is welcomed to the finish by her children.

Kirsten Bey receives a congratulatory welcome on the fly from Race Marshall Al Crane.

Kirsten entered the race just to see the country and pretend to be in the "old days," and finished 13th.

Jeff Darling was the last official finisher, coming in fourteenth. Photos of Jeff by Donna Morgan.

Jeff Darling poses with his leaders after finishing the race. Photo by Donna Morgan.

Mike Santos scratched when he had issues with young dogs; he drove the team back to Nome.

Hugh Neff scratched when his support and supply team experienced major problems on the trail.

ALL ALASKA SWEEPSTAKES

ALL ALASKA SWEEPSTAKES

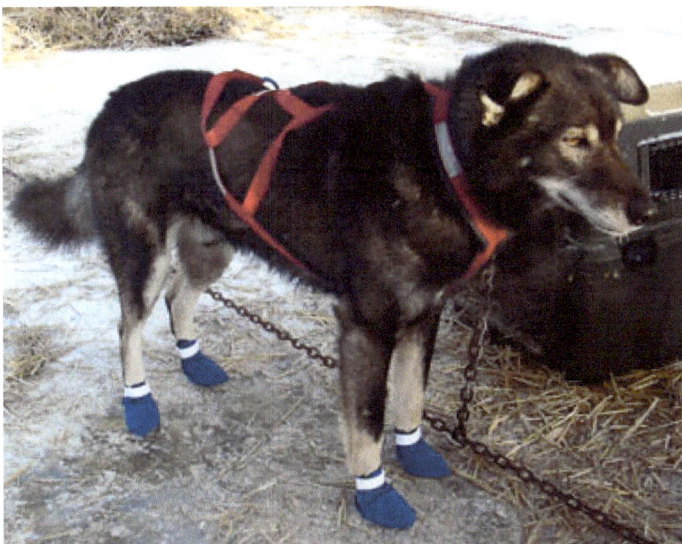

Lance Mackey's Zorro

Ten miles from the finish line in Nome, Lance Mackey's team was hit from behind by a speeding snowmachine. His prized foundation sire, Zorro, who had been riding in the sled bag when the snowmachine struck the sled, was seriously injured. The force of the impact drove the sled thirty feet down the trail, sucking the wheel dogs and the first two team dogs back under the sled and into the tangle of sled, dogs, and snowmachine. A second driver helped Lance untangle the frightened dogs. Not finding any serious injuries and feeling it best to get his team back on the trail, Lance continued to the finish line in Nome, placing third in the race. He was unaware that Zorro had been seriously hurt.

A press release from race officials: *Not until hours after his arrival in Nome did Lance realize that his dog "Zorro" was injured and contacted the race vet team. "Zorro" was stabilized for a flight via Alaska Airlines for continued emergency care in Anchorage and has now been transferred on to Seattle, Washington for continued care and diagnostics.*

With time and excellent care, Zorro recovered, but due to his injuries, he never raced again.

ALL ALASKA SWEEPSTAKES

"It was the most fun I've ever had, I think, in a race!"

"It was the most fun I've ever had, I think, in a race! It was really neat, I enjoyed it immensely! The atmosphere was so great, and the people of Nome were so into it, much more than the Iditarod. It was their race, they had done it, financed it to an extent, put in all the trail work and everything, so the people of Nome were really into it. And then my team... I had so much confidence in that team, even though it was a smaller team, it's just fun running a really nice dogteam, even if you don't win, it goes well and they run well, and they do their job... And having the pit crew out there was awesome! You've got your buddies to talk to. The rules were no talking or helping or pacing between checkpoints, but at the checkpoints they can do everything, so you've got people to talk to and they can do your chores and you can get a little more sleep than you normally would... It was just a nice race that way."
-Mitch Seavey in an interview with *Mushing Magazine* publisher Greg Sellentin, June 6, 2008

ALL ALASKA SWEEPSTAKES

Chapter Six: The Legacy

"Every artfully-crude chandelier in the big room was ablaze with electric candles; club pennants of green and gold bordered the peeled log walls and hung from paintings of champion dog teams, from the mounted heads of moose and polar bears, and from the timbered ceiling. Wide-armed chairs, deep and soft in their upholstering of tanned moose-hide, squatted about the walls. Divans covered with orange fox robes sprawled before a huge cobblestone fireplace in which the blue-and-yellow flame of driftwood flickered, fitfully lighting the crudely lettered motto above it: Life ain't in holding a good hand, but in playin' a poor hand well.

"Down the middle of the room ran the table, splendid, exotic, in its gleaming silver and crystal, with a centerpiece of crimson carnations banked in a three-foot golden cup--the famous Sweepstakes Trophy in which each year the winner of the race was handed his prize money. ...Further decorations ran from this bowl of victory--the long-neck-chains made of grains of raw gold anchored to feminine place cards with little nuggets, and alternating green ribbons pinned to the men's cards with the golden head of a malemute."
        -from The Trail Eater, by Barrett Willoughby

121

ALL ALASKA SWEEPSTAKES

The banquet tables are ready. The menu recreated the Sweepstakes dinners of olden days.

The All Alaska Sweepstakes finish banquet was held in the Nome Recreation Center.

The National Anthem was sung a capella.

Miniature Sweepstakes trophies adorned the tables.

ALL ALASKA SWEEPSTAKES

ALL ALASKA SWEEPSTAKES

Leo Rasmussen and Dr. Phil Schobert

ALL ALASKA SWEEPSTAKES

Jon Van Zyle signs Sweepstakes posters

Connor Thomas signing posters

Cari Miller signing posters

Fred "Moe" Napoka signing posters

ALL ALASKA SWEEPSTAKES

Laura Samuelson, Director of the Carrie McLain Museum

Jayson Russell pays tribute to his grandfather, Pete MacManus, Honorary Musher No. 1

Dr. Denise "Denny" Albert, Lead Veterinarian

Judges Mark Nordman and Joe May

Howard Farley and Dr. Phil Schobert

Race Marshall Al Crane

Mitch Seavey with lead dog Payton

Sweepstakes Awards Banquet

All Alaska Sweepstakes Banquet Night

April 1. 2008, Nome, Alaska

written by Al Crane, Race Marshall

With news from the trail that Jeff Darling, on a lifetime quest, planned to complete the race the following day, mushers and a sellout crowd were treated to a festive awards banquet at the Nome Recreation Center. Guests were treated to a program including a vintage menu. Mushers were recognized and awarded various honors including awarding the top 10 mushers nearly $50,000 raised in the historic Queen contest - this in addition to Mitch Seavey's $100,000 prize.

The evening was made even more special when Laura Samuelson, the director of the Carrie M. McLain Memorial Museum, informed the audience that several relatives of early Sweepstakes participants had been in Nome to celebrate the centennial festivities. The great granddaughter of Johan Hegness, Carrie Shelley, delivered a suitcase full of memories and photographs to the museum and announced that Hegness' ashes, who died in 1960, would be moved to the Nome cemetery. Hegness was the first 1908 Sweepstakes winner.

The museum was also contacted by a grandson of Harry Lawton, who also entered the first race. In 1909, Scotty Allan won the race and Percy Blatchford was 2nd. Percy's granddaughter, Ruby Hollembaek, was in in the audience and recognized by Mrs. Samuelson. The Blatchford family awarded the Blatchford Spirit of the Race Award to Cari Miller of Nome. Percy also ran the race in 1910 and 1912. In 1910, 1911 and 1912, Carl Charles Johnson ran the race. His children, Gene Johnson, Helen McClellon, and Lillian Stevenson from Montana, were in attendance. Charles came in 3rd in 1911 and 1912.

Fred Haswell, great nephew of Esther Birdsall Darling, author of the famous "Baldy of Nome" books and from the Scotty Allan and Darling racing team, who won in 1909, 1911 and 1912, were also recognized in the audience. Maja Ramsey, the granddaughter of Leonhard Seppala, who won three Sweepstakes races, created the Leonhard Seppala Heritage Grant Award in 2005, which awards $10,000 to a worthy rookie musher to run the Iditarod for the first time. In keeping with the spirit of the event, Mitch Seavey donated $10,000 of his earnings to the Leonhard Seppala Grant.

In another interesting highlight, Penny Evans and Alan Bowering of the Siberian Husky Club of Great Britain, which was responsible for returning the 1910 Sweepstakes trophy to the Nome Museum, were also in attendance.

In a very poignant moment at the awards ceremony, Jayson Russell paid tribute to his grandfather, honorary musher No. 1, Pete MacManus. Pete and most of his dogs perished in an airplane accident on his return home from the 1983 All Alaska Sweepstakes Race. Pete's grandsons, Jayson Russell and Pete MacManus Jr., drove the No. 1 team out of the chute to the end of Front St. at the race start.

The finale of the evening came when Mitch Seavey's lead dog, "Payton," was awarded a garland of yellow and green, a symbolic honor steeped in an old tradition - green and gold (yellow), the Nome Kennel Club colors, and the recognition beginning when Iron Man Johnson's record breaking team crossed the finish line in 1910. The crowd threw a horseshoe of flowers around his neck. He removed them and placed them on the leaders of his team, "Kolyma" and "Sandy," declaring "I didn't win the race, the dogs did."

Janice Doherty, All Alaska Sweepstakes Queen, reigned over the entire event.

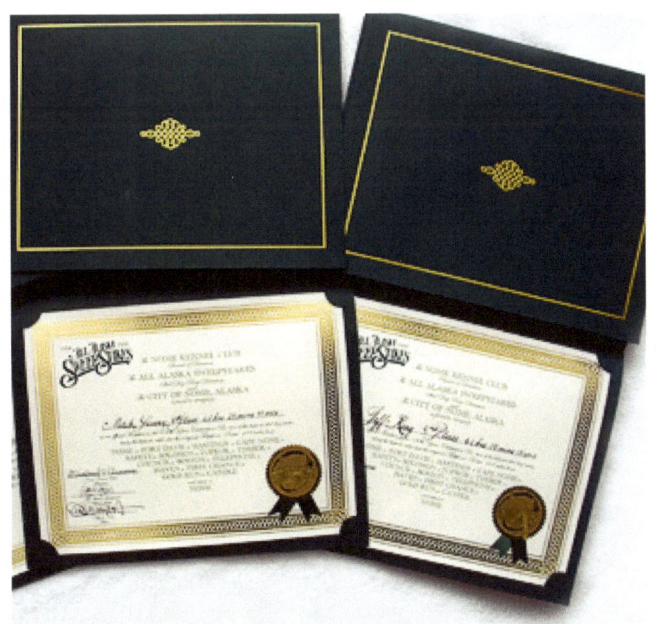

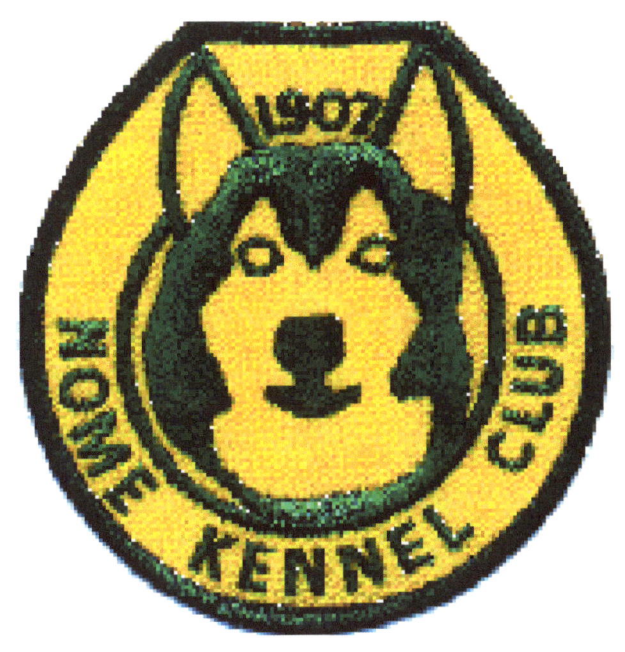

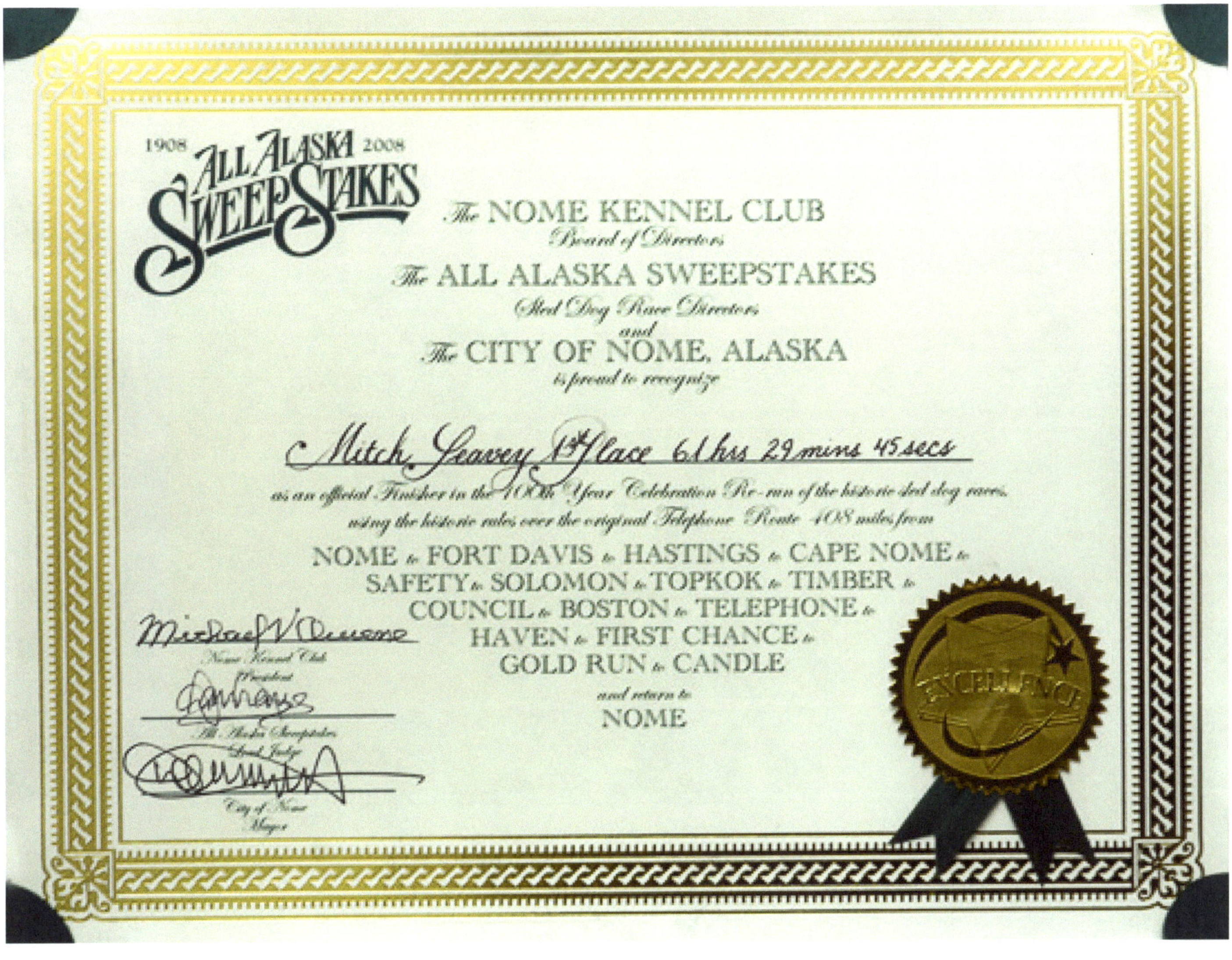
1908 ALL ALASKA SWEEPSTAKES 2008

The NOME KENNEL CLUB
Board of Directors
The ALL ALASKA SWEEPSTAKES
Sled Dog Race Directors
and
The CITY OF NOME, ALASKA
is proud to recognize

Mitch Seavey 1st Place 61 hrs 29 mins 45 secs

as an official Finisher in the 100th Year Celebration Re-run of the historic sled dog races,
using the historic rules over the original Telephone Route 408 miles from

NOME to FORT DAVIS to HASTINGS to CAPE NOME to
SAFETY to SOLOMON to TOPKOK to TIMBER to
COUNCIL to BOSTON to TELEPHONE to
HAVEN to FIRST CHANCE to
GOLD RUN to CANDLE
and return to
NOME

Nome Kennel Club
President

All Alaska Sweepstakes
Head Judge

City of Nome
Mayor

EXCELLENCE

ALL ALASKA SWEEPSTAKES

Percy Blatchford "Spirit of the Race" Award

Percy Blatchford was in the first All Alaska Sweepstakes race; his partner being the now-famous dog driver Scotty Allan.

At her family weblog, titled *Blatchford Herman Ningeulook*, Ruby Hollembaek (daughter of Gloria Blatchford) wrote a wonderful description of the special Percy Blatchford *"Spirit of the Race"* Award which she presented at the Awards Banquet.

Ruby had each of the mushers rise and stand as she read the dedication:

"In memory of my grandfather, Percy Blatchford's love of his dogs and loyalty to the sport of dog racing, we as a family, felt it was important to recognize a musher in his name during this great event. We would have loved to have given an award to every musher and their team, however, we are only able to give a single contribution of $1750 to one musher and dogteam.

"In his memory and with our love, the Blatchford family awards the 'Percy Blatchford Spirit of the Race Award' and $1750 to cover entry fee costs for the 100th Anniversary of the All Alaska Sweepstakes in recognition of the dedication, love and determination and spirit of dog racing, to musher Cari Miller."

ALL ALASKA SWEEPSTAKES

Allen Alexander "Scotty" Allan Humanitarian Award presented to Sonny Lindner

The Allen Alexander "Scotty" Allan award, decided by the race judges and veterinarians, is presented to a musher who has shown excellence in dog care throughout the race. Along with this respected award the musher receives 1,500 pounds of Dr. Tim's Pro Momentum Dog Food.

Allan Alexander "Scotty" Allan was one of the most famous mushers in Alaska in the early part of the century, and was an especially good dog trainer. He dominated the earliest All-Alaska Sweepstakes races. His autobiography, *Gold, Men and Dogs*, includes his service in World War I, when he trained 450 sled dogs for the French military to use in the Alps and the Ardennes, and the Alaskan huskies served quite successfully.

Sonny Lindner, of Two Rivers, has enjoyed a long and illustrious mushing career, winning Iditarod Rookie of the Year in the 1978 race, receiving the Sportsmanship Award in 1979, being named the Most Inspirational Musher in 1999, placing second in the Iditarod in 1981, and winning the first Yukon Quest in 1984. In 2003 he received the Iditarod Sportsmanship Award again, and he's placed in the Iditarod top ten a number of times over the years. Sonny was the recipient of the Humanitarian Award for the 2008 Centennial All Alaska Sweepstakes.

A. A. "Scotty" Allan and Baldy

Sonny Lindner

Below: "Scotty" Alexander's All Alaska Sweepstakes team

ALL ALASKA SWEEPSTAKES

Sweepstakes Queen Janice Doherty and website administrator Theresa Daily

Second place finisher Jeff King receives a big hug from Sweepstakes Queen Janice Doherty

Cari Miller onstage with one of her daughters, sharing stories from the Sweepstakes trail

Janine Seavey watches as her husband Mitch accepts the Sweepstakes check for $100,000.00

ALL ALASKA SWEEPSTAKES

Mitch Seavey accepts the First Place check for $100,000.00 from All Alaska Sweepstakes Queen Janice Doherty and Executive Director Dr. Phil Schobert

ALL ALASKA SWEEPSTAKES

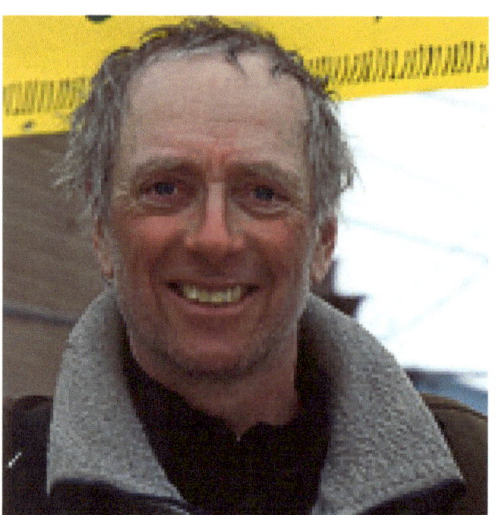

Finisher's Buckle

Fred Moe Napoka

Connor Thomas

Tales of the Trail: The Finishers' Speeches

Each musher came up to the stage and accepted a beautifully framed certificate, a purse from the Sweepstakes Queen contest was awarded to the second through ninth place finishers, and each said a few heartfelt words to the appreciative crowd. A few memorable highlights of what was shared that evening.

In 13th place, Kirsten Bey: She said the race was "just a thrill of a lifetime trip and I'll never forget it! The dogs were incredible... I had a team of young dogs and I just feel like I was so fortunate this year to get this together and thank you to everybody that helped me accomplish it."

In 12th place, Cari Miller: "I'd like to thank my family, especially Brian, he basically supported me through this whole thing and encouraged me, when the times got rough he'd kick me in the butt and say 'get out there' and he and my son Michael... they were both helping me, I couldn't have done it without them. I think this is a memory we'll always cherish. All of my children, like Mary, here at my side, whether it was feed the dogs or cleaning up the dog yard, no matter what it was she was right there, and a valuable asset to my team."

In 11th place, Connor Thomas: A checker in the 1983 Sweepstakes race, Connor was enthusiastic: "What a race! The weather... and I don't think I've never had as much fun in a dog race as this one was; I loved seeing the country."

In 10th place, Fred Moe Napoka: "I had one dog that I had to put in the basket, and he rode from Safety to Candle to Nome, and it seemed like he was howling my name, howling 'Moooe...' and when I first heard him I said 'What did you say? and every time we got to a checkpoint he'd get louder--it was a wonderful race, and I thank all of you!"

In 9th place, Aaron Burmeister: "One of the pilots in Candle asked me if I'd seen any wolves, and I said no, and he said there was a big pack of wolves headed this way. I was about two hours out of Candle on my way to Gold Run and I see all these green eyes about fifty feet off the trail, a hundred yards ahead of me. So I had my headlight on bright and I'm looking at these eyes... My .44 was in my sled so I unzipped my sled bag and I'm looking, there's a lot of sets of eyes looking at me, and as I'm getting close my dogs are picking up speed and a couple of their tails went up and one of the dogs barked and now we're really cruising, so I know there's really something there and I'm not seeing things, and I'm looking really close, and I looked over and there was Fred! He was on his way to Candle and I was on my way back, and he didn't have a headlamp on! And the dog that was 20 feet behind the other ones was curled up in his sled sticking his head out! So Fred, I'd just like you to know you kept me awake all the way to Gold Run! And I've got to compliment you on your beautiful fur parka, it was wonderful to see you out there in that, it's very cool, an awesome parka!"

In 8th place, Ramy Brooks: "I'd like to say thank you to the organization... for putting on a wonderful race, and I think that this race, of all the races I've ever run, really exemplifies what it's all about. ...Wonderful checkpoints, and the Queens raising the money for all the contestants other than first place, and the whole community raising $100,000, just extraordinary..."

ALL ALASKA SWEEPSTAKES

In 7th place, Cim Smyth: "Thank you for putting on this race... [missed the name} put up the gold for the race... I was over to his place for dinner and got to talking about the race and I mentioned that I didn't know where I was going to get the gold... so he started scrounging around in his cupboards, and he came out with a couple of little nuggets, and next he came out with a little handful of dust, and a little more dust, and a couple more nuggets, and pretty soon I had a bunch of little packages of gold, and he put it on the table, and he said, 'Here! You're from Big Lake, you ought to know what an ounce is...'"

In 6th place, Jim Lanier: "There were signs coming into Council for each musher, and mine was 'Re-Run Jim...' I never dreamed before this race that I would be one to break the all-time record, but apparently I did. And I don't want to sound anything but humble about this, however, before the race I told my wife Anna, and during the race I told Mark Nordman, that I had made a study of Seppala's run in 1916, and I planned my race after that run. I did exactly what Seppala did, I stopped the same places and I rested approximately the same length of time. So I thought if I followed that schedule with my dogteam and if we had a pretty good trail, I could trace the race. And that's what I told them, and... And I did! I actually out-Seppalaed Seppala!"

In 5th place, Ed Iten: "Well, after the Iditarod I was laying in bed for two and a half days with a sore back, just didn't think I'd be able to run this race, so I went home, and looked at a few more dogs, and finally got to moving around a little bit and just decided there's no way I could miss it. I'm ever so thankful that I did come back and do the race, it was just a real treat! I don't think we'll ever get four days of the weather we just had again..."

Aaron Burmeister

In 4th place, Sonny Lindner: A man of few words, Sonny accepted the 4th place finisher's Queen's Purse of $6,441.00 from Princess Dana Sherman with a hug, and he commented as she left the stage, "I would'a voted for her...

In 3rd place, Lance Mackey: A longtime friend of the Mackey family, Theresa Daily, read the following letter from Lance, who was on a plane to Seattle to be with his injured dog, Zorro:

"I want to start by saying what a wonderful group of people to be affiliated with. It was an honor to be part of the 2008 All Alaska Sweepstakes. I am very, very sorry I could not be with all of you tonight. I have a family member in serious condition who needs Tonya and I with him.

I want to thank the community for all the help and support in our time of need. I wish to thank all the people who made the most incredible start chute I ever went out of. At one point it seemed to be only three feet wide, hands were hitting both shoulders trying to high five as I passed by, and the excitement of the crowd brought tears to my eyes. It truly was an unforgettable memory for me and my team, and I thank you for that. It was an unexpected end to a great year of racing. I hope this event happens again in the near future. I will definitely be part of it. I want to congratulate all the mushers and their dogs. Great job to all!"

Cim Smyth

Jeff King

The Second Place Runner-Up

In 2nd place, Jeff King, share at the Banquet:

"We took a break at Robert Thompson and Amos' camp on Telephone, and it was a pretty interesting evening. A large gray wolf lay dead outside the wall tent of the checkers, smoke was coming out of the woodstove, and they were both very generous and friendly, and as I took care of my dogs, my crew showed up, and we had a chance to go in and try musk ox stew with these guys..."

"Amos Thompson and his father were enjoying that checkpoint. When I went in the tent finally to warm up, I was freezing, I'm chilled to the bone... I went inside and Amos had no shirt on, from the waist up he was naked! I introduced myself and said who are you? And he said, 'Oh, I'm Amos, this is my dad...'"

"And Robert started telling me that he, Robert, had been a checker 25 years ago at Telephone, and he was glad to be there again. Amos had told me he was 18 years old. A little while later and he said 'Well, I was there too.' And, I'm not that good at math, but I was pretty sure something didn't add up. And I looked at Amos kinda like... You're 18... 25 years ago... I looked at him kinda blank, and he keeps looking at me and he goes, 'Well, I had a tail then.' I was stunned! And I laughed so hard I almost fell on the floor!"

"And that was the beginning of a couple of hours of some of the worst jokes I've ever heard in my life! And I'm pretty sure that I'd have won the race if I hadn't gotten into this joke contest with these two guys... But I guarantee I'm gonna remember some of 'em for years to come..."

Jeff King at Council, by Jan DeNapoli.

Jeff King and Glen Pardy at the Timber Checkpoint. Photo: Sue Steinacher.

Jeff King's team coming into the Council checkpoint. Photo by Jan DeNapoli.

ALL ALASKA SWEEPSTAKES

ALL ALASKA SWEEPSTAKES

Mitch Seavey

The First Place Finisher

2008 All Alaska Sweepstakes Champion

Mitch Seavey on the trail

In 1st place, Mitch Seavey:

"Late in January I was still deciding whether I wanted to try this race or not, and it just so happened that Janie and I were in the airport waiting area, and wanting to get on a flight to go to another race, and another musher asked me 'You think you're gonna win that Sweepstakes?' and I said, 'Well, you know, after the Iditarod and everything, and in the spring, and I know my back's usually kinda sore, and I'm busy... if I run that 408 mile race up there I don't know if I'll be enjoying it too much out there.' And this musher looks at me and says, 'You gotta get over that!' And I said "Yeah, I guess you're right!' So, that musher was Jeff King, and I appreciate that!

"[Payton] is the best sled dog I've ever had, without exception. He's one of those special lead dogs that never gets tired of being in front, he just seems eager to go at all times. You know, on this race it was a challenge for a lead dog, to go through checkpoint after checkpoint, every ten, fifteen, twenty miles there's a checkpoint to go through, and there was varying numbers of legs, and people on snow machines and weaving over obstacles for the leaders to find their way through, and this little bugger would look for the hole and shoot for it, and all he wanted was out of town and back on the trail, and I know without a doubt, we wouldn't have won that race without this dog."

Mitch Seavey

Mitch Seavey leaves the Council checkpoint, headed for Nome. All photos these pages by Jan DeNapoli.

ALL ALASKA SWEEPSTAKES

ALL ALASKA SWEEPSTAKES

Long-time sled dog race fan Marcia Claesson lives in Nebraska, but her passion for the sport of mushing had her joining other race fans online in several Internet forums following the All Alaska Sweepstakes. In this essay she shares her experiences of enjoying the race from afar:

Fans From All Over the World

By Marcia W. Claesson

Sled dog fans aren't just in Alaska. "Arm chair mushers" follow races obsessively from all over the world, frantically hitting F5 to refresh the stats, checking every website we can find, and discussing the races in on-line forums and chat rooms. Mushing enthusiasts form strong bonds with each other, forged through late-night, sleep-deprived conversations out in cyberspace.

One of my favorite places to "hang out" is the mushing forum sponsored by the Bering Strait School District (http://mushing.bssd.org/forum/). The "Idita-buddies" (as we call ourselves) not only discuss the races (and other aspects of our lives), we have contests, host our own "awards banquets," write poetry, and crack jokes.

One of the best "threads" during the 2008 Iditarod started when a poster asked about a musher named "Trail Breaker" who showed up on the GPS and had such a "clear lead so early." After someone informed the original poster that Trail Breaker was a snowmobile breaking trail, the jokes and puns went on for 31 pages, including complex tales about the "Breaker family" with members such as "Ice Breaker," "Jaw Breaker" and "Wind Breaker."

When the Iditarod ends, we all feel a sense of loss, not only because of the end of the race, but because we must say good-bye to the Idita-buddies. But in 2008 we didn't despair, because we had the historic All Alaska Sweepstakes to look forward to.

While waiting for the race to begin, we amused ourselves with another contest (top five picks), and a literary challenge: See how many of the Sweepstakes checkpoints you can use in a story.

Once the race finally started, it was back to sleepless nights and those fascinating cyberspace discussions as we checked race stats.

But following the Sweepstakes was different. No GPS on the screen for this race; we were relying on sometimes sketchy ham radio coverage, but it added an intrigue to the race. As one of the Idita-buddies, known as "dilli," said: "I'm kind of liking the intrigue, romance and patience this information black hole situation is conjuring up. It reminds me of the good old days before instant info and instant gratification became the status quo."

"Breeze" said: "Waiting and wondering used to be a HUGE part of following the Iditarod, so here we are, kinda 'back to the future.'"

As the leaders neared the finish on Friday night, we began to speculate on the estimated finish time for the winner. Thinking it could be as early as 8:00 p.m. Alaska time, we decided to meet in the forum chat room at that time.

Because we have followers from literally all over the world, we schedule our chats in Alaska time, since it's the only time zone we're all familiar with.

Promptly at 8:00 p.m. (11:00 p.m. my time in Nebraska), the Idita-buddies began to gather. Fortunately it was a Friday night, so most of us could sleep in the next day. We had no idea how long of a night it would be.

The usual gang was there. We know ourselves mostly by our forum names. Besides myself (known as emwcee), the Idita-buddies in the chat room included people with forum names such as Heidi, Di, fladogfan, flowerpower, libby the lab, sugarriver, sc-race-ran, tanglefoot (who sometimes goes by tangles), emwcee (that's me), and lower48fan. Someone named "Scott Davis" remained signed in the entire time but never participated; our guess is that it was a teacher left over from the teacher placement chat, who had never logged out. We joked that it was kind of like Joe Runyan's GPS that was still beaming its signal from Nome for weeks after the Iditarod had ended.

At first the chat was mostly about the race itself. We discussed the issue of the start time differential, who we wanted to win, the latest race reports. We joked about how many browser windows we had open on our computers.

Sugarriver had 14. Between two pages for chat, the Sweepstakes standings page, the Iditablog, two cams and the KICY page, I had at least 6 open.

KICY, a radio station in Nome, had coverage of the race finish, but their low bandwidth only allowed for 10 listeners. I kept the window open just in case I would get lucky, but flowerpower was the only one in the chatroom who had coverage, so we relied on her updates.

ALL ALASKA SWEEPSTAKES

Tanglefoot-who lives in the UK--decided to go back to bed, since it was early morning his time. As the evening turned into early morning, we continued talking about our common interests: mushing books we'd read, mushers we'd met personally or would like to meet, Idita-buddies we'd met personally. As the night wore on, we began discussing our pets, our jobs, who we liked on American Idol, what we were snacking on, how tired we were . . .

At one point the server kicked us all off chat. Most of us found our way back on, and the conversation continued.

As we began to feel more sleep deprived, we began pulling practical jokes. Someone said the standings showed Lance Mackey into Fort Davis ahead of the others, and we all scrambled to find the standings page, only to discover it wasn't true. Someone else said the web cam showed a crowd gathering, but that was also a joke.

About 2:00 a.m. my time Tanglefoot joined us as he was getting ready to go to work, then again from work, using a laptop in the pub where he worked. Flowerpower gave us the word from KICY: Mitch was outside of Nome. Things were getting exciting!

Then flowerpower lost KICY coverage. Josh Rogers at the Iditablog site said, "I hate to do this to you, but with King and Seavey getting into Cape Nome just a little bit ago (still minutes apart), I've got to get down to Front Street for the live KICY broadcast."

We were in the dark, with only the Nome web cams to rely on for information!

Someone said, "Dogs! I see dogs!"

We all checked the webcam in time to see a dog team on the street. Ten minutes later we saw another dog team. It was obviously close, but who came in first? We had no way of knowing.
We were frantic. How could we get any info?

This wasn't fun anymore. Someone had won the race, and we had to know who. One of the Idita-buddies typed, "Somebody call Breakers Bar."

I opened yet another browser window, looked up the number, and went to the phon
e. The bar was noisy when I called. "Who won the race?" I asked the lady who answered the phone.

"Mitch Seavey!" she yelled back. I tried to ask how close the finish was, but the bar was too noisy for her to hear me, so I hung up and went back to the computer.

By that time Heidi had already called the Nome Police Department, gotten the news and relayed the info to the group. We finally knew who won. One by one, the fans signed off and went to bed. It was 3:00 a.m.

I thought it was pretty strange that I had called a bar in Nome , Alaska, at 3:00 a.m. my time, from Lincoln, Nebraska. But what happened that morning to tanglefoot, whose real name is Matt Hammersley, was even stranger.

Marcia wrote: Matt lives in Cotswolds, England, where he and his girlfriend maintain a kennel of eight Siberians. They mush on snow as well as dryland, and he has won several races. He's also an avid fan and active Idita-buddy. Here's his story in his own words:

It was one chilly morning in 2008 that I needed a hand, desperately! The 100th anniversary of the All Alaska Sweepstakes Sled Dog Race was coming to a close.

Like many others around the world, I'm HUGE fan of the sport, and the Sweepstakes was the final Hurrah at the end of an amazing season of races, of sleepless endless nights sitting in front of a computer, emailing friends, missing meals to check stats, making my girlfriend a mushing widow and keeping the same run (work) rest schedules as the mushers, to Lance's double race win, following the big races overseas in the "Mecca" of Alaska.

ALL ALASKA SWEEPSTAKES

 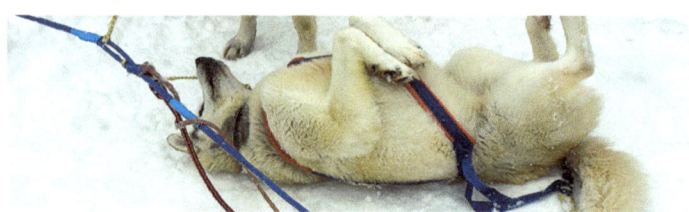

  I had been up most of the night, as I had been most of the past week, F5ing the stats as we call it, dialing into every mushing blog website and online radio station I could find. By then the KTUU newscasters had become as familiar to me as the BBC news anchors in the UK.
  But who was going to win -- Lance, Jeff or Mitch?
  It was getting close. Reports slowed down as Alaska went to bed and the United Kingdom was just waking up. My coffee was keeping the eyes open, and the excitement was building, but...
  I had to be at work. Luckily the pub I was working in had wireless internet, so I hit the coffee machine button again, fired up the work computer, hoping the boss wouldn't be in till late, so I could catch the finish coverage from KICY radio and the webcams on Front Street.
  The computer whirred to life, booted up (should that be bootied up?) and automatically logged into the net. I dialed up the race websites and logged into bssd.org. It was getting close.
  From the UK, Alaska is more than a few thousand miles away -- and yet as close as a click of the mouse.
  I couldn't sit still; the leaders were spotted a short way up the trail from Nome, and the radio presenters were discussing who might pull in first. Five more miles to go... Was it Mitch? Someone said it looked like Jeff.
  Then it happened. The cam went off-line. Oh no! You're joking! Not now... bloody computer... more coffee, more pacing.
  That's okay. The radio was still up and broadcasting, so I could at least hear what was going on. But then it happened. The worst thing happened for us mushing fans listening as the winner got closer to town. The radio must have reached the limit of their bandwidth and went offline. Oh ****!!!
  I tried F5-ing... nothing. Reloading... nothing. Restarting the computer, which seemed to take forever... still nothing. Everything was down.
  I managed to log on to bssd and everyone else was panicking too. It was all down north of White Mountain. So we were robbed of the final moments and who won the 100th anniversary of the race.
  There must be a way to find out who had pulled into Nome. There had to be!
  From somewhere in the ether, "Heidi" from the bssd board had mentioned that she had once spoken to the Nome Police Department to find out the winner of the Iditarod. I wonder...
  I was in fact desperate. I had to know who was winning or had won by now. So I fired off a personal message to Heidi, and she came back a few minutes later with a number, which I think she had gotten from someone in Norway.
  Before I could stop myself, I was dialing the number. I waited... click... waited... a funny tone... then it was ringing...
  I was calling Nome, Alaska!
  A lady answered the phone. "Hello, Nome Police Department, how can I help?"
  She must have thought someone had had too much to drink on Front Street as I stuttered in slight surprise: "Errr... hello... um... I'm calling from England in the UK, and I was wondering if you could tell me who won the Sweepstakes."
  "Sorry, can you repeat that, please. You're calling from where?" came the lady police officer's voice.
  "I'm calling from the UK where the Queen of England lives, and I was following the Sweepstakes from the UK online, and the Internet has gone dead, just before the winner crossed the line, and I wondered if you could tell me who's won?"
  Silence. There was an air of confusion as she tried to come to terms with the call she was taking, and as I thought, Oh, crap, I'm gonna be told off for wasting police time now.

  But the lovely policewoman instead shouted out, to what I guess was a bunch of policemen sitting around drinking coffee: "Hey, guys, there's a man from England, where the queen lives! He wants to know who won the race!"
  "Mitch Seavey! Mitch Seavey came in a few minutes ago. He had a great looking team as well, fresh looking. I think Jeff's gonna be in next... Hang on, did you say you were following the race from England?"

"Er, yes, ma'am," I replied. "I'm a musher too and well, I wanted to know who won, as the Internet died. So Mitch won?"

"Yes, he did!" She came back sounding amazed and now as excited to be chatting with someone in the UK as I was to be talking to her in Alaska.

"Yes, he did! He looked great! You're a musher in the UK? Really? How many dogs, er, I mean, do you get snow?"

This was amazing! Here we were discussing dogs. How many did Mitch have? How did they look coming in?

We talked all about where I lived in the UK, my dogs, how we mush, the races we have won. The policewoman said she had always wanted to come to England. We chatted for a good half hour about the country she lived in and where I lived. Every now and then, she would shout to the others in the room bits of information about my dogs in the UK.

She asked the others in the room if Jeff had come in yet, told me how the crowd on Front Street was ten deep and only a gap wide enough for Mitch and his swift team of huskies to break trail through the lot of them to get to the finish line and how he got mobbed by the crowd.

It was fantastic! Through this wonderful, wonderful lady I could have been there on Front Street!

We finished the call, as I was worried the boss would arrive and I'd get the sack. I thanked her so much for letting me know who won. I don't know what her job was there, but I can't thank her enough for the time she took to tell me all about her town, Mitch's team coming in and a little bit about life in Alaska.

So through fans of this amazing sport from Norway to the USA -- and a wonderful policewoman in Nome, I got to hear how Mitch had won. This sport of ours once again showed me that no matter where in the world we live, we are a community and ready to lend a paw at the drop of a musher's hat. Isn't that great?

So, when I finally get to Nome, Alaska, be it by dogsled or airplane, one of the first things I'm going to do is call the police station and see if the lovely lady is around and thank her in person.

I'm sorry I've forgotten your name, but if you're the person who answered the phone from a mad mushing fan from the Queen's England, thank you! You saved my sanity! If you ever to make it to the UK, look me up. I owe you a beer!

Late Night with the Sweepstakes

A poem by Marcia W. Claesson
(from the Central Time Zone point of view)

It's 11 pm and we're in chat,
Wondering where the teams are at.
There's Heidi, Di and fladogfan,
Who's Scott Davis, do you know the man?
An unsigned out teacher, that's my guess.
Just like Joe Runyan's GPS.

It's 12 a.m. and we're in chat,
Wondering where Jeff and Mitch are at.
Tangles just went back to bed,
Flowerpower and Libby are here instead.
What's the latest from Josh's blog?
How's Lance doing without his lead dog?

It's 1 a.m. and we're in chat,
Wondering where the leader's at.
Sugarriver and sc-race-fan
Are sharing tales of the Breaker clan.
Meeting a musher would be a treat,
Meeting an Idita-buddy would be sweet!

It's 2 a.m. and we're in chat,
Wondering where the winner's at.
Lower 48's here and Tangles is back,
John even came to join the pack.
We're sleep deprived and playing pranks,
A report that Lance has joined the ranks.

It's 2:30 a.m. and we're still in chat,
Wondering where the info's at.
There must be problems with the ham,
Then we see two dog teams on the cam!
Heidi says, "I'm calling Nome.
We anxiously wait for her to phone.

It's 3:00 a.m. and we've leaving chat,
Now we know where the winner's at.
Mitch Seavey has won the race,
A worthy musher gets first place!
The Idita-buddies can go to bed
While visions of sled dogs dance in their heads.

ALL ALASKA SWEEPSTAKES

Jodi Bailey, of Chatanika, Alaska, designed and updated the All Alaska Sweepstakes leaderboard which kept things running smoothly for race fans, officials, and the mushers' crews. An instructor for the Interior Aleutians Campus of the University of Alaska, Fairbanks, Jodi is a champion musher, and shares a kennel with partner Dan Kaduce, an Iditarod and Yukon Quest finisher. In a post on her webblog the evening of the Sweepstakes banquet, Jodi wrote:

The Finish Banquet

by Jodi Bailey

Wednesday, April 02, 2008

Well, the race is run and tonight we all sat down to celebrate it. The finish banquet held at the Nome rec center was a big event. The food was delicious, and the menu was based on one of the original finisher's dinners: Salmon with herbs, garlic mashed potatoes, bacon wrapped tenderloin, peas with pearl onions. There were macaroons and ladyfingers for dessert, and cheese and crackers to keep us going as the evening progressed.

It was a wonderful time to also give recognition to all the many people who made a race like this possible. Colby (head of SPARCS ham radio club) was a true gem. Always the gentleman, he made a point of thanking all the HAM operators who made communications on this very long remote trail a reality. The race organization was very kind in thanking all the 'media' types, and they gave Theresa Daily a plaque of appreciation. I want to publicly thank her, because without her I would never have had the opportunity to be here for this historic event. Also want to give a shout out to Mark and Helen at Northern Light Media (check them out to buy the new Lance Mackey DVD) and Donna at Husky Productions, I am glad to have had the chance to get to know them and I was lucky to be working around such fun and interesting folks.

There was a humanitarian award given for dog care in honor of "Scotty" Allan, it was well deserved by Sonny Lindner. I have already mentioned how impressed I was with the commitment and friendship that went into the agreement with Rick Swenson. And I was very happy to see excellence in mushing (dog care, conditioning and team management) honored at this historic event. Considering the caliber of teams and mushers, it is even more of an achievement to be honored; congratulations, Sonny!

Speak of the great Scotty Allan, what a character worth learning more about. His biography is the out of print *"Gold, Men, and Dogs,"* the story of his life in his words, and a great first hand account of the sweepstakes from Scotty's (the winner's) perspective. As a champion with multiple runs in the race he has a great story to tell, whether it is charging Topkok Hill in a blizzard with creepers (crampons) on and Baldy in lead, or his observations on his competition and the nature of fame:

"Thurstrup (a driver with a Siberian team owned by Goosak) got in the next morning. And I was there to meet him, and when I saw the small crowd, compared to the night before, it killed for the time being the joy of winning the race. Here was a man that had gone through far more than I had - over seven hours longer on the trail, with very little rest and running a loosing race practically from the start. If he had not been a man of iron and grit he would never have finished." (Allan, *"Gold, Men, and Dogs,"* p. 195)

ALL ALASKA SWEEPSTAKES

I like that last section of Allan's book, it illustrates what I call the "Miss America moment," where you are out there working your ass off to win. But at the same time you respect, heck in a lot of cases even really like the person you are up against. So really you are both out there, each of you totally aware of what it took to get that far, the commitment, effort and investment. You want all the best for that person here next to you, you just want to do better, and there is no way to do that... but at their expense. A strange dynamic. But as Allan's narrative illustrates (and by the way I see it over and over in the races we go to) Honor among thieves pales in comparison to honor among mushers. So to all the mushers who can now proudly join the very short list of All Alaska Sweepstakes finishers, *CONGRATULATIONS!!!*

One last musher deserves a special note: Jeff Darling. He was still out on the trail as we ate our fancy food, shared stories and basically sat warm and comfy (did I mention that right now in Nome we are having a freezing wet snow / verging on rain thing, very nasty). The cold and wet and never say quit Darling hopes to finish his Sweepstakes tomorrow evening. What probably nobody knows, because as far as I can tell he would never make a big deal of it, is that Jeff has MS. His commitment to his sport and this race is really inspirational, and although I fly out tomorrow (weather permitting), I leave a wish that Jeff has continued safe travels.

Our future Red Lantern in the 2008 Sweepstakes deserves all of our support and good vibes as he finishes his run to Candle and back to Nome. I am told that the Nome City Council will bring the burled arch back out for his return, the fire siren will sound, and considering what I have seen of Nome I expect a enthusiastic crowd to greet him.

Happy trails,
Jodi

Posted April 3, 2008 at the Northern Light Media blog:

The airport in Nome was crowded with people associated with the race in various ways: mushers, judges, pilots, checkpoint crews, media crews - many with gathered families and supporters... And the plane waiting for all of us on the runway was Alaska Airlines' famed "Salmon-Forty-Salmon."

Everyone was on the plane and getting comfortably settled when Theresa Daily got a phone call and announced that Jeff Darling was in Safety! We all applauded his progress and left Nome delighted to know that he was finally so close to home and his Sweepstakes finish. We hoped a good crowd would be there to meet him, and several of us admitted we'd thought about staying for a later flight and probably would have if we'd known he was so close.

Fast-forward to Anchorage. A large group is gathered in the concourse to say good-byes before heading down to gather baggage and go on their separate ways. Race Marshall and Lead Judge Al Crane takes a phone call from Nome: Jeff Darling is 100 yards from the finish line!

Al held up his cellphone and the dozen or so people standing in Anchorage cheered him to the finish line from 1,000 miles away! Jeff was clocked under the burled arch at 11:56:11 for a total elapsed trail time of 169:56:11, taking the red lantern and 14th place.

It was a very fitting finish to a great race, and we all left the airport in Anchorage knowing the last musher was safely home in Nome!

ALL ALASKA SWEEPSTAKES

Notes, Appendix & Bibliography

In the photo above, Fred Moe Napoka, coach of the Tuluksak School team, poses with his lead dogs and young Alayah Kunnuk of Nome, while Tuluksak School principal Mariah Thomas-Wolf looks on. Alayah, who greeted almost every finishing musher, is wearing a parka which belonged to her grandmother, and was made over fifty years ago by her great-grandmother.

The Centennial All Alaska Sweepstakes was full of stories like Alayah's, and like Moe and Mariah's story - they brought the only public school sled dog team in the U.S. to the Sweepstakes race, from a small rural village about sixty miles north of Bethel, on the Kuskokwim River. The school's special education instructor and cheerleading coach, Brita Steinberger, wrote in a letter, "Tuluksak is a village on the Southwest Alaskan tundra with a population of 428. The school is 99.3% Alaskan Native (Yupi'k Eskimo). The native population maintains a subsistence lifestyle, primarily living from hunting and gathering, as they have for thousands of years. The village does not have plumbing or running water. Despite this inconvenience, Tuluksak has a strong sense of community and really comes together behind the dog team."

In his musher's profile Moe explained a little more: "Tuluksak School is the only school in the country that has a dog-sled team as part of our school curriculum. Our principal wanted our school team to run the All Alaska Sweepstakes to honor Pete MacManus who was a school teacher and musher. We were hoping to get a student to run the team, but that didn't work out due to state testing which begins on April 1st. Instead, she asked me to run the team with the support of three Tuluksak students (Crim, Leroy, and Nicholai), my brother Jacob, the principal Mariah, her husband Craig, and her son Zack. Our dogs are from Martin Buser's Happy Trails Kennel: leaders Iris, Angus, Lewis, and Jack; team dogs Eva, Liberty, Bug, Io, Siv, Callisto, Clark, and Harlem. Thanks to our sponsors: We are in the last year of a 5-year grant from the YKHC Diabetes Prevention Program, Eagle Pack dogfood, Prairie Bilt Sleds, Cabela's, Grant Aviation, Arctic Transportation Services, JP Air, Northern Air Cargo/Alta Air Logistics."

Compelling stories accompany every sled dog race, but the historic All Alaska Sweepstakes Race brought together some wonderful personal stories, like those of Sweepstakes Queen contestants Merdith Ahmasuk of Nome, the youngest daughter of Harold Ahmasuk Jr., who ran the race in 1983, and finished; or Dana Sherman, whose father, Jake Sherman, traveled from their home in Candle to Nome for the exciting 1983 race, with his mother, Dana's Ahna Lizzie, and little Dana in tow. Dana wrote, "I was only 11 months old at the time, but still enjoy the stories of having been there for it; my first race."

ALL ALASKA SWEEPSTAKES

ALL ALASKA SWEEPSTAKES

2008 ALL ALASKA SWEEPSTAKES BOARD

Race Officials:

Race Director: Dr. Phil Schobert of Nome
Assistant Race Director: Lisa Schobert

Race Marshal/Lead Judge: Al Crane was the 1983 All Alaska Sweepstakes lead judge, past president of Nome Kennel Club & Iditarod Trail Committee and top 20 finisher in the Iditarod Sled Dog Race. He has been Race marshal/judge for the Iditarod, the Alpirod, and the Coldfoot Classic to name a few.

Race Judges: Supporting Al Crane are race judges from across the state. Nels Alexie from the Kusko 300, Al Marple from the Copper Basin, Mike McCowan from the Yukon Quest & North American, Mark Nordman from the Iditarod, Chuck Schaffer from the Kobuk 440 & Jerry Tokar from the Fur Rondy and the only other surviving race judge from the 1983 All Alaska Sweepstakes. Joe May, 1980 Iditarod race champion, will act as an alternate race judge.

Lead Veterinarian: Dr. Denise Albert has worked as a trail veterinarian on marathon sled races for 13 years. These include numerous Iditarods, Wyoming Stage Stops and many other mid and long distance races. She has served as chief veterinarian for races in Minnesota and South America.

Trail Veterinarians: Dennis Griffin, Tex Coady, Susan Whiton, Caroline Griffitts, Paul Pifer & Turner Lewis
Communications Director: Siobahn Bradley
Awards Ceremony: Sue Christenson
Checkpoint Coordinator: Sue Steinacher
Banquet Coordinator: Susanne Thomas
Banquet Chef: Tim Stettenger
Banquet Designer: Liz Murphy
Queen Coordinator: Kristen Timbers
Volunteer Coordinator: George Bard
Housing Coordinator: Sari Haugen
Trail Air Transportation Coordinator: Stan Morgan
Membership & Trail Mail: Leo Rasmussen
Web Design: Theresa Daily
Emergency Services: Liz Recchia
Merchandising: Erica Pryzmont
Nome Kennel Club President: Mike Owens
Official Photographer: Jeff Schultz
Video Documentary: Husky Productions
Book Production: Northern Light Media
Official Artist: Jon Van Zyle
Attorney: Conner Thomas
Historian: Laura Samuelson
Fund Raising: Urtha Lenharr
Musher Registration: Lisa Schobert
Trail Coordinator: Mitch Erickson
Official Timer: Leo Rasmussen

Race Marshall Al Crane and All Alaska Sweepstakes Queen Janice Doherty

ALL ALASKA SWEEPSTAKES

Tuluksak School Principal Mariah Thomas-Wolf

World sled dog race champion Roxy Wright

Kirsten Bey receives a warm welcome home.

Jim Lanier and Dr. Phil Schobert

ALL ALASKA SWEEPSTAKES

Volunteers & Supporters

The true unsung heros of the race are the many people who took the time and made the effort to help make this race happen, and the sponsors who made it all possible:

Diana Adams
Meredith Ahmasuk
Harold Ahmasuk
Janet Ahmasuk
Frank Anderson
Jane Anderson
Daniel Anderson
Ray Ashenfelter
Jodi Bailey
Chester Ballot
Kelly Blevins
John Bockman
Charlie Brobst
Daniel Brugleria
Michele Burke
Paul Burke
Lance Cannon
John Carpenter
Josie Coppock
Theresa Dailey
Peggy Darling
Jan DeNapoli
Janice Doherty
Tom Ellana
Mike Evans
Shoni Evans
Chuck & Peggy Fagerstrom
Sheri Fagerstrom
Mark & Marcia Fairbanks
Julie Farley
Harvey Fiskeaux
Martha Fiskeaux
Mary Fiskeaux
Anna Fiskeaux
Susie Fiskeaux
Melissa Ford
Bev Geizer
Tammy Gologergen
Stacy Green
Fletcher Gregg Jr.
Major Grennon
Delores Guilliam
Lester Hadley
Stacy Hafner
John Handland
Joe Hannah
Jim Hansen
Kay Hansen
Sari Haughen

Mark & Helen Hegener
Seji Heck
Dionne Herman
Karina Hernandez
Carlee Hobbs
Kristina Hoffert
Bill Howell
Dora Hughes
Becky Irish
Karlin Itchoak
Brian James
Stephanie Johnson
Lance Johnson
Robin Johnson
Colleen Johnson
Sharon Keeney
Dr. Mark Kelso
Kevin Klott
Dr. Bob Lawrence
Vic Lawyer III
Charlie Lean
George Leckband
Dr. Leedy
Martina Leedy
Ron Locke
Adam Lust
Peter Macmanus
Bob Madden
Dr. Owens Mandanas
Charlotte Mathias
Sandra Medearis
Earl Merchant
Lisa Merchant
Carl Merchant
Debbie Merchant
Denise Michaels
Marry Miller
Donna Morgan
Elizabet Murphey
Louis Murphey
Dodi Nesbit
Kendra Nichols
Annie Kate Olson
Barb Olson
Dr. Karen O'Neill
Myrna Outwater
Michael Owens
Melissa Owens
Mike Owens

Pat Owens
Glen Pardy
Pam Parnell
Christina Parrigo
Ray Peterson
Steve Pomrenke
Chris Pomrenke
Andy Potter
Erika Pryzmont
Phil Pryzmont
Donna Quante
Erna Rasmussen
Leo Rasmussen
Carlin Rauch
Mary Reader
Caroline Reader
Cussy Reader
Josh Rogers
Fred Ross
Jason Russell
Buford Sallaffie
Gary Samuelson
Laura Samuelson
Zack Schindler
Dan Schobert
Katie Schobert
Millie Schobert
Dana Sherman
Nick Sherman
Robert Sherman
Jenny Shield
Sharon Sparks
Tom Sparks
Dan Stang
Maggie Stang
Tim Stettinger
Dan Sullivan
Delbert Thomas
Mariah Thomas
Suzanne Thomas
Roger Thompson
Kirsten Timbers
Roseann Timbers
Lew & Loki Tobin
Ken Upchurch
Tom Vaden
Lisa Wehde
Brandon Wehde
Dawn Wehde

Cecilia Wehde
Jon Wehde
Brian Weinard
Larry Westlake
Dempsey Woods
Robyn Woyte
MayJo Zuelsdorf

HAMS

Colby Carter
Ramon Gandia
Char Keehn
Bob & Kathy Douglas
Pat Hahn
Bonnie Hahn
Randy Oles
Ken Shapiro
Jim Stimpfle
Eric Morris
Nate Perkins

Sponsors

Nome Community Center
AMI Crew
Wells Fargo
Alaska Airlines
NAC
Momentum
Alaska Gold Company
NSEDC
Bering Air
GCI
Rasmussen Music
Nome Public School
Daily's Web Design
Bonanza Express
Apocalyps Design
Crowley
Taiga

ALL ALASKA SWEEPSTAKES

The Companion DVD:

Running With Spirits
The 2008 All Alaska Sweepstakes

Video by Donna Quante, Husky Productions

    It was the richest purse ever offered for a long distance sled dog race: $100,000.00 winner take all! The top mushers of the day brought their mandatory pokes of gold and signed on for the historic run: Lance Mackey, Jeff King, Mitch Seavey, Sonny Lindner and fourteen others left the starting chute on Front Street for the 408-mile run across the remote Seward Peninsula to Candle and back. They'd be running trails made famous by Leonhard Seppala, "Scotty" Allan, "Iron Man" Johnson, and many other renowned Alaskan mushers. They'd be running with the spirits of the greatest sled dog races ever held.

    This is a two hour commemorative DVD, produced by multiple Emmy award-winning videographer Donna Quante, tells the colorful story of the centennial running of this iconic race in 2008, when the townspeople of Nome successfully recaptured and recreated all of the excitement and thrilling history of the gold rush era in Alaska.

    Hauntingly beautiful original music by Kyf Brewer and Jim Parkinson highlight this video journal of the 2008 All Alaska Sweepstakes. Donna's camera takes the viewer behind the scenes as mushers get ready for the race, following the special events associated with the historic running, and counting down the exciting start as the spectators recreate the historic "human chute" to see the mushers off. Mark Hegener's stunning video footage of each team leaving the start line puts the viewer right in the action, while Donna Quante's and Jan DeNapoli's shots and footage follow the teams out of the chute and out of town, onto the Bering Sea. Then the story moves to the checkpoints out on the trail, showcasing some of the most desolately beautiful country in Alaska.

    Interviews with checkpoint volunteers, veterinarians, pilots, judges and the mushers themselves give an insider's perspective and a feeling for what it was like to be in Nome during this incredible time. Wrapping up the whole marvelous visual package is the viewer's ticket to the All Alaska Sweepstakes banquet, with many heart-warming surprises and delights in the Sweepstakes Awards Ceremony. The film is supplemented with incredible still photography from master photographer Jan DeNapoli, who shares her experience at the Council checkpoint. "Running with Spirits" captures all the excitement, the history, and the ongoing legacy of Alaska's premier sled dog race.

To order, contact Husky Productions, PO Box 1085, Willow, AK 99688.
http://www.huskyproductions.net

Dog lot on the edge of the Bering Sea

Ivory carvings in a window

Leonhard Seppala's leader, Fritz

Bibliography, Sources and References

Allan, Allen Alexander. *Gold, Men and Dogs*. New York & London: G. P. Putnam's Sons, 1931.

Cole, Terrence. *Nome: City of the Golden Beaches*. Anchorage: Alaska Geographic Society, 1984.

Coppinger, Lorna; *The World of Sled Dogs: From Siberia to Sport Racing*. New York: Howell Book House, 1977.

Darling, Esther Birdsall. *Baldy of Nome*. Philadelphia, PA: Penn Publishing Co., 1916.

Darling, Esther Birdsall. *Navarre of the North*. Garden City, NY: The Sun Dial Press, Inc., 1930.

Darling, Esther Birdsall. *The Great Dog Races of Nome: Official Souvenir History (1916)*. Knik, Alaska: Iditarod Trail Committee, 1969.

Ferrell, Nancy. *Barrett Willoughby: Alaska's Forgotten Lady*. Anchorage: University of Alaska Press, 1994.

Garst, Shannon. *Scotty Allan: King of the Dog-Team Drivers*. New York: Julian Messner, 1946.

Hawkes, Clarence. *Silversheene, King of Sled Dogs*. New York: Platt & Munk Co., 1918.

McLain, Carrie. *Gold Rush Nome*. Portland, OR: Graphic Arts Center, 1969.

Murphy, Claire Rudolf and Jane G. Haigh. *Gold Rush Dogs*. Anchorage: Alaska Northwest Books, 2001.

Rennick, Penny, ed. *Dogs of the North*. Anchorage: Alaska Geographic Society, 1987.

Ricker, Elizabeth M., with Leonhard Seppala. *Seppala: Alaskan Dog Driver*. New York: Grosset & Dunlap, 1930.

ALL ALASKA SWEEPSTAKES

Ricker, Elizabeth M., with Leonhard Seppala. *Togo's Fireside Reflections.* Lewiston, ME: Lewiston Journal Printshop, 1928.

Salisbury, Gay and Laney. *The Cruelest Miles: The Heroic Story of Dogs and Men in a Race Against an Epidemic.* New York, W.W. Norton & Company, Inc., 2003.

Standiford, Natalie. *The Bravest Dog Ever: The True Story of Balto.* New York: Random House, 1989.

Stephenson, William B. *The Land of Tomorrow.* George B. Doran, New York, 1919.

Stuck, Hudson. *Ten Thousand Miles with a Dog Sled: A Narrative of Winter Travel in Interior Alaska.* New York: Scribner's, 1914; Lincoln & London: University of Nebraska Press, reprinted 1977, 1988.

Walden, Arthur T. *A Dog-Puncher on the Yukon.* Boston and New York: Houghton Mifflin Company, 1931.

Willoughby, Barrett. *Alaskans All.* Boston and New York: Houghton Mifflin Company, 1933.

Willoughby, Barrett. *The Trail Eater, A Romance of the All-Alaska Sweepstakes.* New York: G. P. Putnam's Sons, 1929.

Wirt, Loyal Lincoln. *Alaskan Adventures: A Tale of Our Last Frontier, and of 'Whiskers', Gallant Leader of the First Dog Team to Cross Alaska.* New York: Fleming H. Revell Co., 1937.

Web Sites for the All Alaska Sweepstakes

http://www.allalaskasweepstakes.org
http://northernlightmedia.com
http://mushinghistory.wordpress.com
http://www.baltostruestory.com
http://www.xalaska.com/sweeps/boston08.html

Jim Lanier

Lance Mackey's ID tag

Front Street, Nome

Index

15 Mile Camp...87
1910 Sweepstakes trophy...128
1925 diphtheria epidemic...18, 22, 24
1983 Sweepstakes poster...27
1983 Sweepstakes...26, 50, 52
2008 Sweepstakes poster...31

~ A ~

accident, Lance Mackey...119
Adams, Diana...152
Ahl, Kevin...79
Ahmasuk, Harold Jr....148, 152
Ahmasuk, Janet...152
Ahmasuk, Meredith...41, 148, 152
Alaska Airlines...152
Alaska Gold Company...152
Alaska Railroad...24
Albert, Dr. Denise...37, 126, 150
Alexie, Nels...35, 81, 150
All Alaska Sweepstakes coin...30
All Alaska Sweepstakes Queen...11, 34, 40, 53, 56, 79, 108, 109, 113-115, 120, 128, 134-136
Allan, George...18
Allan, Allen Alexander...10, 14, 17, 21-24, 28, 30, 82, 109, 131, 146
Allen Alexander "Scotty" Allan Humanitarian Award...132, 133
American Kennel Club...23
AMI Crew...152
Anchorage Daily News...104
Anderson, Daniel...152
Anderson, Frank...152
Anderson, Jane...152
Andy...26, 27, 55
Apocalyps Design...152
Appetite and Attitude...10, 146
Ashenfelter, Ray...106, 152
Awards banquet...120-147

~ B ~

Bailey, Jodi...11, 90, 146, 152
Baker's...17
Baldy of Nome...21, 41, 43, 79, 82, 128, 133, 146
Ballot, Chester...152
Bard, George...150
Berger team...19
Bering Air...152
Bering Strait School District...142
Bey, Hawker...54
Bey, Kirsten...42, 51, 54, 55, 59, 69, 78, 116, 136, 151
Blatchford Blues, The...21
Blatchford Spirit of the Race Award...128, 130, 131
Blatchford, Gloria...131
Blatchford, Percy...128, 130, 131
Blevins, Kelly...152
Board of Trade Saloon...11, 22, 30, 105
Bockman, John...106, 152
Bonanza Express...152
Bondarenko, Anna...137
Boston...17, 85, 106
Bowering, Alan...128
Bradley, Siobahn...150
Brewer, Kyf...151
Brobst, Charlie...152
Brooks, Ramy...51, 57, 61, 74, 79, 114, 136
Brown, Les...90
Brugleria, Daniel...79, 152
Brynteson, John...32
BSSD...142
Burke, Michele...152
Burke, Paul...152
burled arch...5, 32, 110, 111
Burmeister, Aaron...39, 51, 55, 59, 66, 78, 82, 114, 136
Burmeister, Mandy...114
Buser, Martin...148
Butcher, Susan...26, 55

~ C ~

cabin, Seppala's...33
Camp Haven...104, 106
Candle...17, 18, 20, 26, 40, 41, 85, 98-102 104, 106, 121, 136, 147, 148
Cannon, Lance...152
Cape Nome...17, 32, 85, 106
Carpenter, John...104, 152
Carrie McLain Museum...99, 126, 128
Carter, Colby...90, 146, 152
champions, past races...28
checkpoints...46, 49, 84, 85, 93, 95, 96
cheechako...21
Chief...27
Christenson, Sue...150
Claesson, Marcia W....142, 145
Coady, Tex...37, 150
coin, All Alaska Sweepstakes...30
color guard...123
companion DVD...151
Coppinger, Lorna...22, 53
Coppock, Josie...152
Council...6, 7, 17, 18, 82-89, 91, 93, 96, 97, 104, 106, 138-141, 151
Crane, Al...24, 35, 50, 106, 112-117, 128, 147, 150
Crane, Jo...106
Crim...54, 148
Croix de Guerre...21
Crowley...152

~ D ~

Daily, Theresa...10, 11, 90, 137, 146, 147, 150, 152
Daily's Web Design...152
Dalhousie, Lord...21
Dalzene, Fay...22, 28
Darling, Esther Birdsall...7, 18, 28, 41, 43, 79, 128
Darling, Jeff...9, 43, 51, 56, 60, 71, 78, 117, 128, 147
Darling, Mrs. C.E....21
Darling, Peggy...56, 152
Death Valley...18, 104, 106
Deering...101
DeNapoli, Jan...11, 151, 152
Diamond Anniversary Race...26
Ditka...110
dog collar, leather...30
Dog Derby...20
dog lot...47
Dog Races of Nome, The Great...28
dog yard...48
dogs, famous...21, 27, 55
Doherty, Chrystiene...40
Doherty, Doug...36, 40, 79
Doherty, Janice...40, 41, 45, 108, 113-115, 120, 128, 134, 135, 150
Douglas, Bob...152
Douglas, Kathy...152
Dubby...21
DVD...151

~ E ~

Eggart, Larry...36, 100, 101
Ellana, Tom...106, 152
Erickson, Jim...79

Erickson, Mitch...150
Evans, Mike...152
Evans, Penny...128
Evans, Shoni...152

~ F ~

Fagerstrom, Chuck...100, 102, 152
Fagerstrom, Peggy...100, 102, 152
Fagerstrom, Sheri...152
Fairbanks, Marcia...103, 152
Fairbanks, Mark...103, 152
Fairhaven Hospital...98, 100, 102
Farley, Howard...24, 47, 106, 127
Farley, Julie...152
Finish banquet...120-147
Finisher's certificates...129, 136
Finishers' Purses...11, 15, 21, 26, 129, 136, 137
finishing time...129
Fink, Albert...15, 20, 21, 28
First Chance...17, 54, 85, 106, 115
Fish River...17
Fiskeaux, Anna...152
Fiskeaux, Harvey...152
Fiskeaux, Martha...152
Fiskeaux, Mary...152
Fiskeaux, Susie...152
Follies, Nome...46
Ford, Melissa...106, 152
Fort Davis...17, 32, 85, 105, 106
Fritz...22, 23, 154

~ G ~

Gandia, Ramon...106, 152
GCI...152
Geizer, Bev...152
Gold Run...17, 85, 100, 106, 136
Gold Rush Dogs...82
Gold, Men and Dogs...30, 133, 146
Gologergen, Tammy...41, 152
Goosak, William...16, 146
Governor's Declaration...32
Granite...55
Great Dog Races of Nome, The...18, 28
Green, Stacy...152
Gregg, Fletcher Jr....152
Grennon, Major...152
Griffin, Dennis...37, 150
Griffitts, Caroline...37, 150
Guilliam, Delores...152

~ H ~

Hadley, Lester...106, 152
Hafner, Stacy...152
Hahn, Bonnie...106, 152
Hahn, Pat...106, 152
Haigh, Jane G....82
Halter, Vern...55
HAM operators...146
Hammersley, Matt...143
Handland, John...152
Hannah, Joe...152
Hansen, Jim...152
Hansen, Kay...152
Hartman, Diane...106
Hastings...17, 85, 106
Haswell, Fred...128
Haugen, Sari...150, 152
Haven...17, 85
Heck, Seji...152
Hegener, Helen...10, 119, 146, 152
Hegener, Mark...2, 10, 11, 78, 90, 119, 146, 151, 152
Hegness, John...21, 28, 128
Herman, Dionne...152
Hernandez, Karina...152
Hobbs, Carlee...152
Hoffert, Kristina...152
Hollembaek, Ruby...128, 130, 131
Honorary Musher No. 1...52, 126, 128
Howell, Bill...152
Hughes, Dora Mae...41, 114, 152
Humanitarian Award, 1983...26, 54, 132, 133
Husky Productions...146, 150, 151

~ I ~

Internet...142
Irish, Becky...106, 152
Itchoak, Karlin...152
Iten, Ed...39, 51, 54, 58, 65, 78, 93, 112, 137
ivory carvings...154

~ J ~

Jack McMillan...21
James, Brian...152
Johnson, Carl Charles...128
Johnson, Colleen...152
Johnson, Gene...128

Johnson, John "Iron Man"...16, 22, 24, 28, 99, 128. 105, 108, 128, 151
Johnson, Johnny...11, 90
Johnson, Lance...152
Johnson, Lawrence...106
Johnson, Robin...152
Johnson, Stephanie...106, 152
judges...35, 50, 80, 81, 106, 126
Junes, Rodney...79

~ K ~

Kalma...21
Keehn, Char...105, 106, 152
Keeney, Sharon...152
Kelso, Dr. Mark...152
Kid...82
Kineen, Simon...36, 84, 91
King, Jeff...6, 38, 43, 51, 56, 60, 70, 78, 93, 99, 104, 105, 111, 134, 138-140
Klott, Kevin...90, 104, 152
Kolyma...16, 128
Kunnuk, Alayah...148

~ L ~

Lanier, Jim...11, 43, 48, 51, 53, 54, 58, 64, 78, 94, 113, 137, 151
Lanier, Jimmy...113
Lawrence, Dr. Bob...152
Lawton, Harry...128
Lawyer, Vic III...100, 103, 152
leaderboard...10, 11, 12, 19, 101
Lean, Charlie...106, 152
leather dog collar...30
Leckband, George...152
Leedy, Dr....152
Leedy, Martina...152
Lenharr, Urtha...150
Leonhard Seppala Heritage Grant Award...128
Leonhard Seppala Humanitarian Award...54
Leonhard Seppala trophy...26
Leroy...54, 148
Lewis, Turner...37, 150
Lindblom, Erik...32
Lindeberg, Jafet...32
Lindner, Ava...112
Lindner, Sonny...3, 26, 27, 51, 57, 61, 77, 79, 86, 112, 132, 137, 146, 151
Locke, Ron...152

Index continued

Lust, Adam...152

~ M ~

Mackey, Dick...26, 57
Mackey, Lance DVD...146
Mackey, Lance...10, 39, 47, 51, 54, 57, 61, 75, 79, 83, 93, 94, 96, 99, 104, 105, 111, 118, 119, 137, 151
Mackey, Rick...57
Mackey, Tonya...137
MacManus, Pete...42, 52, 126, 128, 148
MacManus, Peter...42, 52, 78, 128, 152
Madden, Bob...152
Malamuts...21
Mandanas, Dr. Owens...152
Marple, Al...35, 150
Mathias, Charlotte...152
May, Joe...35, 101, 126, 150
McClellon, Helen...128
McCowan, Mike...35, 106, 150
Medearis, Sandra...152
Medley, Lolly...57
Menu, Finish banquet...146
Merchant, Carl...152
Merchant, Debbie...152
Merchant, Earl...152
Merchant, Lisa...152
Michaels, Denise...108, 152
Miller, Cari...43, 51, 55, 59, 68, 78, 116, 125, 128, 130, 131, 134, 136
Miller, Marry...152
Miller, Michael...43
Mini Convention Center...47, 49
Momentum...152
Moore, Mike...79
Morgan, Donna...106, 152
Morgan, Stan...36, 79, 106, 150
Morris, Eric...152
Morton, Al...87, 106
Moto, Marlene...101
Murphey, Elizabet...152
Murphey, Louis...152
Murphy, Claire Rudolf...82
Murphy, Liz...150
Mushing Magazine...120

~ N ~

NAC...152
Napoka, Fred "Moe"...39, 51, 54, 58, 63, 78, 115, 125, 136, 148
Napoka, Jacob...148
Neff, Hugh...42, 46, 51, 55, 59, 67, 78, 117
Nenana...24
Nesbit, Dodi...47, 152
Nicholai...54, 148
Nichols, Kendra...152
Niuluk River...84, 87, 97
Nome Community Center...152
Nome Follies...46
Nome Kennel Club...15, 20, 24, 26, 28, 50, 92, 109, 129, 150
Nome Nugget 1908...92
Nome Police Department...143, 144
Nome Public School...152
Nordman, Mark...35, 80, 105, 126, 137, 150
Northern Light Media...146, 147, 150
Northern Whites...54
Norton Sound...87
NSEDC...152
Nugget...27

~ O ~

OB...27
Old Buddy...27
Oles, Randy...106, 152
Olson, Annie Kate...152
Olson, Barb...152
Olson, Richard "Red Fox"...32
Ophir Creek...87
Outwater, Myrna...152
Owens, Melissa...152
Owens, Michael...152
Owens, Mike...150, 152
Owens, Pat...152
O'Neill, Dr. Karen...152

~ P ~

Palin, Gov. Sarah...32
Pardy, Glen...106, 107, 138, 152
Parkinson, Jim...151
Parnell, Pam...152
Parrigo, Christina...152
past race champions...28
Payton...110, 128, 140
Peacock, Lanka...79
Peary, Robert...56
Perkins, Nate...152
Peterson, Ray...106, 152
Pifer, Paul...37, 150
pilots...36, 91
Pomrenke, Chris...152
Pomrenke, Steve...152
Potter, Andy...152
Pryzmont, Erika...150, 152
Pryzmont, Phil...152

~ Q ~

Quante, Donna...10, 119, 146, 151, 152
Queen of the North...41

~ R ~

race champions...28
race judges...35
Race Marshal...50, 112-117, 147
Race Officials...150
Ramsay, Col. Charles...15
Ramsay, Fox Maule...16, 21, 24
Ramsey, Maja...128
Ramstead, Karen...10
Rasmussen Music...152
Rasmussen, Erna...152
Rasmussen, Leo...106, 108, 124, 150, 152
Rauch, Carlin...152
Reader, Caroline...19, 40, 44, 152
Reader, Cussy...152
Reader, Mary...152
Recchia, Liz...150
Red Lantern...32, 43, 147
Redington, Joe Sr....27
reindeer...32
Rex...21
Reynolds, Tamara...46, 55
Ricker, Elizabeth...109
Rogers, Josh...90, 143, 152
Ross, Fred...152
Rowe, Chris...106
Rowe, Jim...106
Ruby Derby...28
rules...92
Running With Spirits...151
Runyan, Joe...55
Russell, Jayson...42, 52, 126, 128, 152

~ S ~

Safety...17, 32, 85, 105, 106, 136
Salisbury, Gay...18
Salisbury, Laney...18
Sallaffie, Buford...79, 152

Salmon-Forty-Salmon...146
Samuelson, Gary...152
Samuelson, Laura...99, 126, 128, 150, 152
Sandy...128
Santos, Mike...42, 51, 56, 60, 73, 79, 117
Schaeffer, Chuck...35, 106, 150
Schindler, Zack...152
Schobert, Dan...152
Schobert, Dr. Phil...24, 31, 34, 38, 90, 110, 124, 127, 135, 150, 151
Schobert, Katie...34, 41, 152
Schobert, Lisa...34, 38, 150
Schobert, Millie...152
Schultz, Jeff...150
Seavey, Dan...56, 105
Seavey, Danny...56
Seavey, Janine...134
Seavey, Mitch... 8, 28, 38, 51, 56, 60, 72, 79, 96, 99, 104, 108, 110, 111, 120, 128, 134, 135, 140, 141, 151
Seavey, Tyrell...56
Sellentin, Greg...120
Seppala's cabin...33
Seppala, Alaskan Dog Driver...22, 109
Seppala, Constance...109
Seppala, Leonard...10, 16, 22-24, 25, 28, 32, 33, 109, 128, 137, 151, 154
Serum Run...22, 24
Service, Robert...83
Seward Peninsula Amateur Radio Club...11
Shapiro, Ken...106, 152
Shelley, Carrie...128
Sherman, Dana...41, 137, 148, 152
Sherman, Dorothy...103
Sherman, Jake...148
Sherman, Mike...101, 103
Sherman, Nick...152
Sherman, Robert...152
Shield, Jenny...152
Siberian husky...16, 22, 23, 24, 29, 99, 128
Smith, Kathie...111
Smyth, Bud...57
Smyth, Cim...51, 57, 61, 76, 79, 113, 137
snowmachine accident...119
snowmachines...47, 84

Snyder, Robert...40
Solomon...17, 85, 104, 106
Sookiyak, Marlin...79
SPARC...90, 146
Sparks, Sharon...152
Sparks, Tom...106, 152
Spruce Creek...82
St. Lawrence Island...24
St. Michael...20
Stang family...84, 86
Stang, Al...87
Stang, Dan...106, 152
Stang, Maggie...87, 106, 152
Stefansson, Vilhjalmur...28
Steinacher, Sue...106, 107, 150
Steinberger, Brita...148
Stephenson, William B....20
Stettenger, Tim...150, 152
Stevenson, Lillian...128
Stimpfle, Jim...106, 152
Stuck, Hudson...18, 84
Suggen...16
Sullivan, Dan...152
supplies...46, 91
Swenson, Rick...19, 26, 27, 28, 55, 57, 112, 146

~ T ~

Taiga...152
Team of Husky Men...79
Telephone...17, 85, 106, 138
Ten Thousand Miles with a Dogsled... 18, 84
The Cruelest Miles...18
The Land of Tomorrow...20
The Trail Eater...32, 121
The World of Sled Dogs...22, 53
thirty-three dog team...20
Thomas, H. Connor...38, 51, 54, 58, 62, 78, 115, 125, 136, 150
Thomas, Delbert...152
Thomas, Mariah...54, 148, 151, 152
Thomas, Susanne...150, 152
Thompson, Amos...106, 138
Thompson, Robert...138
Thompson, Roger...106, 152
Three Lucky Swedes...32
Thurstup, Louis...16, 146
Timber...17, 82, 85, 104, 106, 107, 138
Timbers, Kirsten...150, 152

Timbers, Roseann...152
Tobin, Lew...106, 152
Tobin, Loki...106, 152
Togo...22, 23, 25, 27
Tokar, Jerry...35, 150
Topkok Hill...18, 106, 146
Topkok...17, 82, 85, 106
trail breakers...47
Trail Veterinarians...37, 150
Tucker, Ron...27
Tuluksak...54, 115, 148
Tungwenuk, Bruce...79

~ U ~

U.S. Mail...25, 28
Upchurch, Ken...106, 152

~ V ~

Vaden, Tom...106, 152
Van Zyle, Jon...31, 46, 106, 110, 125, 150
Van Zyle, Jona...46, 106
Vaughn, Col. Norman...54
veterinarians...37, 92, 93, 126, 150
video, race...151

~ W ~

Wehde, Brandon...152
Wehde, Cecilia...152
Wehde, Dawn...152
Wehde, Jon...152
Wehde, Lisa...152
Weiler, Jay...36, 79, 91, 106
Weinard, Brian...152
Wells Fargo...152
Westlake, Larry...101, 103, 152
Whiton, Susan...37, 91, 93, 150
Wiliams, Kelly...112
Willoughby, Barrett...16, 18, 32, 121
winning time...121, 129
Wireless Telegraph System...28
Woods, Dempsey...152
World War I...21, 24, 25
World War II...25
Woyte, Robyn...152
Wright, Gareth...57
Wright, Roxy...57, 151

~ Z ~

Zorro...104, 118, 119, 137
Zuelsdorf, MayJo...152

www.ingramcontent.com/pod-product-compliance
Lightning Source LLC
Chambersburg PA
CBHW041518220426
43667CB00002B/28